中国的历史

CHINA
A HISTORY

CHERYL BARDOE

THE FIELD MUSEUM

ABRAMS BOOKS FOR YOUNG READERS

NEW YORK

THIS BOOK WAS MADE POSSIBLE IN PART BY THE ELIZABETH F. CHENEY FOUNDATION AND THE HENRY LUCE FOUNDATION.

Cataloging-in-Publication Data has been applied for and may be obtained from the Library of Congress.

ISBN 978-1-4197-2121-2

ABRAMS The Art of Books
195 Broadway, New York, NY 10007
abramsbooks.com

内
容

CONTENTS

结语
CONCLUSION

For centuries, cranes in China have been symbols of longevity.

展望未来

LOOKING TO THE FUTURE

Today China has almost 1.4 billion residents, a literacy rate of 95 percent, and one of the world's largest economies. In the early twenty-first century, China once again achieved the favorable trade balance—exporting more than it imports—that it held for so long in earlier times. Traditional industries are thriving: Metalworking produces iron pipes, fasteners, and steel cutlery sets. Textile factories produce cotton T-shirts, knit sweaters, and silk scarves. Ceramic goods include plates, mugs, and porcelain sinks. In addition, China is a major producer of computers, telephones, and electrical appliances.

Besides economic growth, the last half of the twentieth century brought a dramatic rise in cities: The coastal city of Shenzhen, for example, was home to thirty thousand in 1980. Just thirty-five years later, it had more than ten million residents.

The breakneck speed of such change has brought China urgent challenges. Systems for workplace safety are still catching up to demanding production schedules. Air and water pollution are major areas of concern, as is soil erosion in the Yellow River valley. Not everyone has benefitted equally from the prosperity—and history has shown that a great divide between the haves and the have-nots eventually brings social unrest. Meanwhile many challenge the modern government's harsh punishments for those who attempt to speak freely.

Issues relating to human rights, the environment, and fair distribution of resources

The Beijing National Stadium, which opened for the 2008 Olympics, is an architectural landmark of modern China.

are at the forefront of twenty-first-century challenges worldwide. Scientists estimate that the world had fewer than ten million people in 10,000 BC, when Neolithic peoples grappled with the switch from living in small, nomadic groups to life in larger settlements. Now the world has more than seven billion people trying to figure out how to live and work together.

The ideas and inventions of China have influenced the world in countless ways throughout history. Even so, the role of China in the world's future cannot be predicted. In China, as everywhere, it will be influenced by the combination of environmental factors, the country's history of decisions, and ongoing, never-ending human ingenuity.

Shanghai, the country's biggest city and a global financial hub, at night.

Over millions of years, erosion has sculpted these limestone rocks. Known as spirit stones, they offer inspiration to contemplate the balance between change and stability over time.

Field Museum curator Berthold Laufer holds a cup made from a rhinoceros horn.

SCHOLARLY INTEREST

Beginning in the earliest Chinese dynasties, past stories were valued for any lessons they could offer to inform present actions. History also played a critical role in how each new dynasty bolstered its authority to rule.

Foreigners also took an interest in China's history, mostly in connection with missionary outreach, trade relations, or the passing fancies of fashion. Western scholarly interest in China began in earnest as the fields of archaeology (the study of past human societies and cultural traditions) and anthropology (the study of human cultures) became better developed in the early 1900s. Swedish scholar Johan Gunnar Andersson's search for China's Neolithic societies was part of this trend. Sir Aurel Stein, from England, led three famous expeditions to rediscover ancient sites along the Silk Road. Berthold Laufer, a German-born American scholar, made his first trip to China in 1901.

From 1908 to 1923, Laufer returned to China on behalf of The Field Museum and collected what would eventually be nineteen thousand artifacts, spanning the Neolithic period to the early twentieth century. Although he was never able to visit Tibet personally, Laufer also purchased four thousand artifacts associated with Tibetan beliefs, practices, and technology.

Like other Western scholars, Laufer greatly appreciated the guidance of Chinese intellectuals, whose knowledge and social manners he described as "the true index of the degree of a nation's civilization."

Berthold Laufer (*far right*) on a 1904 trip to gather artifacts in China.

PREHISTORIC CHINA

CHINA'S STORY BEGINS IN THE STONE AGE

Based on the fossil record, close relatives of modern humans have lived in China for at least seven hundred and fifty thousand years. For most of this time, these hominins—and the modern humans who succeeded them—survived by hunting and gathering. They lived nomadically, moving from place to place and making few changes to the landscape. They struck stones together to shape and sharpen them into tools, so scientists call most of this time expanse the Paleolithic, which means Old Stone Age.

About ten thousand years ago people began building more-permanent homes, dwelling in larger groups, and experimenting with farming. These dramatic changes required new ways of thinking about how to live and work together.

Settled communities physically changed surrounding landscapes, and individuals began making specialties of various tasks. Success brought population growth, constant trying out of new ideas, and increased layers of status in society. People still relied on stone, but now had more techniques—including grinding and polishing—to shape a wider range of tools. Scientists call the years from about 10,000 to 1800 BC the Neolithic, which means New Stone Age.

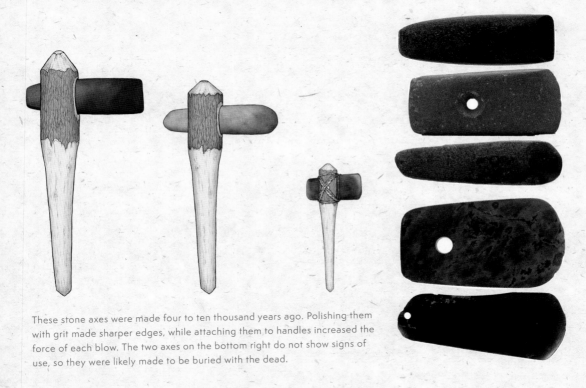

These stone axes were made four to ten thousand years ago. Polishing them with grit made sharper edges, while attaching them to handles increased the force of each blow. The two axes on the bottom right do not show signs of use, so they were likely made to be buried with the dead.

Neolithic peoples invented the building blocks of modern society. Most people today, for example, reside in homes that stay in one place. More live in cities than in the countryside. Most eat farmed food, with diets relying on plants and animals first cultivated by Neolithic farmers. Today people talk about the fast-paced change of technology and how much humans are transforming the environment. Although

such changes in the Neolithic period seem slow by comparison, they were rapid-fire when judged against the steadiness of earlier lifestyles.

The distinct societies that emerged in Neolithic China were the foundation for this nation's diverse population today.

SEEKING THE ROOTS OF CHINESE CIVILIZATION

The Yellow River springs forth in China's northwest mountains and meanders thirty-four hundred miles through the heart of this nation. It slices through lowlands covered in a fine, fertile soil called loess. For millions of years, winds gusting across nearby mountains and deserts have dropped specks of dust on these plains, gradually building loess to a thickness of five hundred feet in some places. It is no wonder then, that this valley attracted some of the world's earliest farmers.

Over time, regular flooding of the Yellow River created flat, fertile plains in the lowlands.

By 2600 BC, villages with thousands of residents existed in China. Farmers in surrounding areas produced surplus crops to trade there.

Marking history back to the first dynasties, scholars traditionally considered the Yellow River valley to be where Chinese cultural traditions or civilization began. It was assumed, however, that humans first made the leap from Stone Age–lifestyles to complex societies farther west. Scholars worldwide used to believe that the level of social organization that is recognized as civilization first occurred around 3500 BC in Mesopotamia (modern-day Iraq) and nearby Egypt. They believed the strategies for lots of people living and working together then spread from this region to the rest of the world, including the territory that today is known as China. A Swedish geologist named Johan Gunnar Andersson, however, wondered if China could also claim a major prehistoric society.

Andersson came to China in 1914, hired by the government to identify geological deposits for mining. He noticed the ancient stone tools sold in the countryside and in 1921 traveled to Henan Province hoping to prove his theory. As Andersson explored the deep ravines rainwater had carved into the loess, he spied a distinct layer of ash and pottery fragments. The pottery was obviously ancient, but Andersson doubted that such advanced technology existed alongside stone tools. "Somewhat dejected," he later wrote, "I felt that I had followed a track which would only lead me astray."

Top: Johan Gunnar Andersson conducted the first modern archaeological excavations in China.
Bottom: He floated artifacts back to Beijing on rafts buoyed by yak skins stuffed with straw.

Andersson found pots similar to these. Scholars don't know whether the painted designs were symbolic or simply decorative.

Pondering this puzzle of pottery kept Andersson up nights. Finding ancient ceramics was nothing new in China. Where others focused on a relic's beauty, however, Andersson documented the depths at which objects were found. Being a geologist, he understood that older layers of earth are usually positioned below newer ones. Thus the deeper the artifacts were buried, the older they likely were. At last Andersson concluded that the pottery did indeed date to the Neolithic period. In the following years, he collected thousands of artifacts and floated them back toward Beijing on river rafts made of branches and yak skins stuffed with straw. His work proved that a complex society existed here thousands of years before China's first dynasty. Suddenly, scholars faced the possibility that Chinese civilization had its own separate roots.

IMAGINE YANGSHAO VILLAGE LIFE SEVEN THOUSAND YEARS AGO . . .

You live in a round house in which wooden poles support thatched roofs and walls made of packed earth. You share this home with your immediate family, and homes for your aunts, uncles, and cousins cluster nearby. The largest home belongs to the head of your extended family. About fifty such dwellings, housing several hundred people, make up the entire village. The door of everyone's house opens onto a central plaza—the hub of community life and the site for important ceremonies and group decision-making. One of your chores is to let pigs out of the thornbush pen that everyone shares at the center of town. The pigs spend the day foraging in the woods and you shoo them back into the pen each night.

Every family in this village does a little bit of everything to make a living. That means every family gathers and grows food, sews clothes with bone needles, fires pots in the kiln, and spends hours grinding stones into axes. For food, you enjoy acorns, sour dates, tubers, deer, rabbits, and fish from the nearby river. You also save an extra supply of millet to survive each winter.

Your town is bounded by a large ditch to help deter any unwelcome visitors or wild animals that want to steal young pigs from their pen. Kilns, another shared resource, are placed on the outskirts of town to reduce the danger of spreading fire. Graves also tend to be outside town limits, and you honor your ancestors by giving them food and a tool to make their way in the afterlife. Graceful, swirling designs adorn some of the pottery in these graves.

Yangshao societies, named for the village where Andersson first collected associated artifacts, thrived from about 5000 to 3000 BC. Today's archaeologists use even more rigorous methods than Andersson's to examine archaeological sites. First, they map an entire site and identify specific spots for excavation. Each area of investigation is then divided into a grid, often marked by crisscrossing strings. A precise grid location and depth from the surface are recorded for each object found. Scientists also read the soil for hints about architecture and activities: dark circles reveal

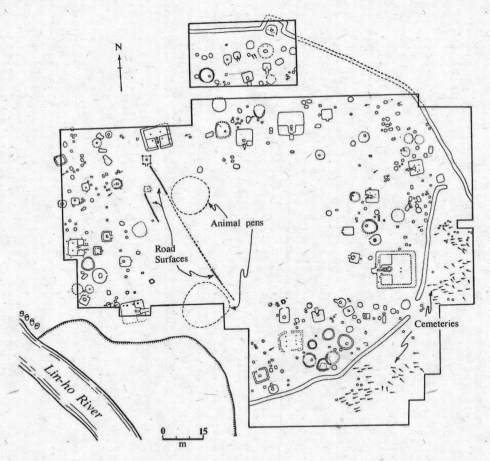

Archaeologists mapped evidence of wooden poles, fires, kilns, and burials to envision this Yangshao settlement near the Yellow River.

where wood from house poles rotted; dark orange patches are evidence of hearths; compacted, smooth soil indicates floors. Ancient trash pits become treasure troves as scientists examine even the broken bits of anything left behind. After carefully documenting all evidence of human activity at a site, archaeologists try to reconstruct ancient ways of living.

MANY CRADLES OF CIVILIZATION

China is now recognized as a place where civilization developed independently—as in, groups of people formed large, complex societies without influence from other large societies, such as Mesopotamia and Egypt. In addition to Yangshao communities, scholars have evidence that dozens of Neolithic societies rose and fell within modern China's boundaries. Today's scholars also recognize other cradles of civilization, including the coast of modern Peru, highland Mexico, and the Indus River valley, which is located in modern Pakistan and northwest India.

Pottery, with its infinite variety of clay, shape, and decoration, offers clues for telling apart groups with different cultural practices. The oldest-known pottery in the

The world's oldest-known pottery fragments. People began making pottery in China even before they settled in villages.

As this Yangshao jar filled with water, the weight kept the jar balanced and upright to prevent spills.

world was found in Jiangxi Province and dates back twenty thousand years—even earlier than the Neolithic period. "Having a vessel to carry things seems like such a simple thing, but it's a really important development," says archaeologist Deborah Bekken, of Chicago's Field Museum of Natural History. "This new technology gave people much more flexibility." Pottery keeps out water and rodents so well that some ancient storage jars found today still preserve grain from long ago. Pottery expands cooking possibilities because it can be placed on flames without catching fire. It also provides a canvas for people to express themselves artistically.

Although ceramic jars made it easier to store extra piles of tiny grains, toting around such heavy, breakable vessels was difficult. Tucking them into the ground just outside a family dwelling was more appealing. Therefore pottery may have encouraged people to stay put rather than move about. Archaeological evidence shows that Neolithic peoples in China probably experimented with living in settled communities *before* they began farming intensively. The switch to permanent homes likely began as people became attached to favorite seasonal sites. A group might have found a fall location convenient for gathering millet from a marsh and collecting fruit from a forest. Perhaps each year the group stayed longer and longer, until eventually people lived there year-round.

In some cases, prehistoric people built up a food surplus, the significance of

which cannot be underestimated. Besides increasing the odds of survival, it changes how people invest their time and energy. "Because you aren't moving around all the time," Dr. Bekken says, "you can create new objects and ways of doing things. This allows for an economy with more innovation."

Farming is another invention people developed independently in China. Plants and animals are called domesticated when they no longer thrive and reproduce without human care. The earliest animals to be domesticated were those already living in social groups and following humans to scavenge food. In China, this first meant dogs, which may have been valued as food, in addition to being hunters, protectors, and companions. Pigs and chickens were next to the fold. "You want animals that are easy to manage, gain weight quickly, and taste good," Dr. Bekken says. "Pigs are particularly efficient at growing and they eat almost anything, so you don't need to plant specific crops to support them."

Farmers still use water buffalo, which may have been domesticated alongside rice about nine thousand years ago.

Top: Rice plant
Bottom: As archaeologists sift soil in water tanks, lighter objects—like ancient seeds and grains—float to the top.

Most wild animals fear humans, but a few individuals in each of these species would have been less afraid, coming closer and closer for food. By befriending and breeding sociable animals, people ended up with packs, herds, and flocks that were comfortable around humans. The domestication of plants also happened at first by accident: Wild grains tend to lose seeds easily in the breeze, and seeds that blow away are difficult to gather. So when prehistoric peoples harvested wild millet and rice stalks, they got grains that were more likely to cling tight during harvesting. By planting these seeds, they ended up with more of the same. Over time, farmers began breeding animals and plants to emphasize desired traits on purpose.

Consequently throughout the Neolithic period, people living in what is now China used the innovations of pottery, settlement, and farming to revolutionize daily life. Yet, with such basic tools, how different could these societies be?

Very.

Environment has always influenced lifestyle. The Yangshao communities

along the Yellow River experienced cool winters and enough rain to grow millet. Meanwhile, seven hundred fifty miles southeast, in the warmer, wetter climate of today's Zhejiang Province, peoples associated with Hemudu cultural traditions farmed the more labor-intensive rice. That environment produced mud thick enough to seal artifacts away from oxygen and the organisms that cause decay. Therefore modern archaeologists have discovered the remnants of many wooden poles, revealing the architecture of Hemudu houses.

The history of group decisions, combined with individual creativity, also leads people to different choices. The Hongshan communities—one thousand miles

In southern China, thick mud preserved Hemudu house posts.

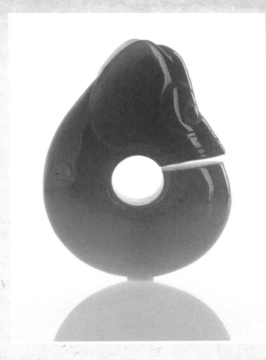

The northern Hongshan society had a thriving industry making jade objects like this modern pig-dragon.

northeast of Yangshao, but also of the same era—are more famous for their jade carvings than their pottery. Researchers are particularly curious about the Hongshan figures called pig-dragons, which have piglike heads and curled bodies similar to a snake's. In many early cultures of China, pigs became a marker of wealth. Although the exact significance of pig-dragons is not known, they may illustrate how practical elements of daily life take on symbolic meanings.

The variety of Neolithic societies matters. "Sometimes people view the history of China as being one long train, moving forward," Dr. Bekken says. "But it was a diverse place from the very beginning." What interests scholars, then, is how so many distinct groups eventually developed shared customs that continue to unify China's diverse peoples today.

Trade is one answer to that question. The movement of people and things has always spurred an exchange of ideas, resources, and information. Even settled Neolithic groups sometimes traveled over land and navigated rivers. Members of Hongshan communities journeyed up to fifty miles to a central temple for rituals and imported jade from mines 180 miles away. They may easily have encountered people with practices and traditions different from theirs on these trips.

Cherishing jade is one custom that likely spread through trade. Although it was mined mostly in two areas—near the Yangtze River in the south and today's Liaoning

Province in the northeast—prehistoric jade artifacts are found throughout China. Jade is the common name for two types of rock, both prized for their ability to be carved and polished to a smooth, lustrous sheen. Nephrite glows in soft grays and greens, while jadeite dazzles with intense greens, pinks, browns, and blacks. Other stones, with characteristics similar to jade, also were used by Neolithic societies in the same way as real jade.

Across Neolithic China, people fashioned jade into pendants, tools, and weapons. Shaping jade required hours of careful labor, so jade objects became symbols

Carved animal symbols appear throughout Chinese history, from the Neolithic period to these jade carvings from the Shang Dynasty.

of wealth and status, used in rituals and accompanying burials. Two kinds of jade objects found in countless graves are *bi* disks, smooth circles with holes in the middle, and *cong* tubes, which are square on the outside and round on the inside.

Silk was another sign of status shared far and wide. A braided belt, thread, and a few woven scraps dating from around five thousand years ago were found in a tomb in Zhejiang Province. More durable tools for making textiles and carvings showing this work have been found in graves at least six thousand years old. Chemical evidence of silk has been found in the soil of tombs that are more than eight thousand years old.

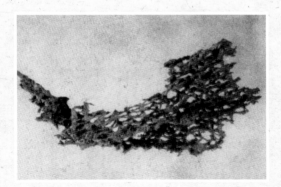

Jade *bi* disks (*top*) and *cong* tubes (*bottom left*) began appearing in graves more than forty-two-hundred years ago. The cong tube may have been thought to link heaven and earth. The bi disks showed the wealth and status of the dead.

The oldest known fragment of silk (*bottom right*) survived in a tomb for almost five thousand years.

IMAGINE HEMUDU VILLAGE LIFE SEVEN THOUSAND YEARS AGO . . .

Your house rises on stilts to escape the floodwaters that chase heavy rains and to improve airflow during hot, humid summers. You share this home, a seventy-five-foot-long rectangle, with an extended family of twenty to thirty people. About ten such longhouses, surrounded by a fence, make up the village. The wooden beams framing these houses are cut precisely so that a tab from one fits snugly into a hole in another. Called a mortise and tenon joint, this precision carpentry is produced by axes and chisels made of stone.

Some days you twist hemp and grass ropes into nets to catch fish in the nearby Yangtze River. Other days you trill bone whistles to lure deer close enough to shoot with bows and arrows. Your village also hunts rhinoceros, tiger, and bear. From nearby forests, you gather acorns, tubers, and fruit. And throughout the growing season, you sweat in rice paddies, leveling soil and carefully flooding fields so that seedlings get enough water to survive, but not so much that they drown.

Each family cares for its own pigs and chickens, corralled into pens behind the longhouses. The well at the center of town, however, is shared. You are so close to the ocean, it is lined with logs to prevent saltwater from seeping in.

Some tools in your village are ground from a dark volcanic rock not found nearby. Someone paddled a wooden canoe down the river to trade for these resources. Perhaps in exchange they offered an unusual ceramic vessel or a wooden bowl made waterproof using sap from the lacquer tree. People in your village know the trick of adding charcoal to clay to make shiny black pottery, and you admire the drawings of plants and animals etched into the clay before it is fired.

THE SCALE OF STONE AGE SOCIETY

It's easy to imagine Stone Age people as being few and far between. Yet archaeologists have identified dozens of Hemudu and Hongshan villages, plus more than one thousand Yangshao settlements. Each location had populations ranging from several hundred to about a thousand residents. And those are just the sites that have been discovered so far.

Studying how populations spread across an area is as important as examining individual sites. This is why Field Museum archaeologist and curator Dr. Gary Feinman helped lead one of the first large-scale surveys of archaeological sites in China. Each autumn, from 1995 to 2008, Dr. Feinman and his colleagues trekked across harvested cabbage and wheat fields, over forested hills, and through mucky wetlands. With five people, each standing about thirty feet apart, they hiked more than one thousand miles along the east coast of Shandong Province, scanning the ground for hints of the past.

By mapping the locations of artifacts across China's countryside, Dr. Gary Feinman documents where and when people lived along China's coast.

Local residents are often interested in the archaeologists' work. Cutaway areas alongside roads can reveal many finds.

These adventures took scientists deep into the countryside, where farmers greeted them with giant radishes and were surprised to see Westerners so far from a city. "I've seen people ride by on bikes," Dr. Feinman recalls, "and just like in cartoons they look so intently at me that their heads turn and their bikes run into trees." Rural areas are excellent places to survey because so little ground is hidden by cement or buildings. Although destructive, plowing does not lead to the complete disappearance of the pottery and tools that archaeologists seek. "Farming churns the landscape enough to bring ancient artifacts to the surface," Dr. Feinman says, "but not enough to totally destroy layers of ancient occupations that were deposited thousands of years ago." Most of the remnants of pottery and tools that Dr. Feinman seeks have already broken over time, so plows cause minimal damage to these artifacts.

What looks like trash to some is a treasure trove of information for archaeologists. Here, Gary Feinman (left) and Professor Fang Hui (right) examine their finds.

Dr. Feinman's trained eyes have spotted evidence of the past in today's modern landscape. The team mapped a lengthy section of an earthen wall that marked a long-lost territorial border. Frequently they have encountered ancient tombs— disguised as low bluffs, with exposed dirt sides and grass-covered tops—poking unexpectedly from otherwise flat farmland. Even if farmers don't know their significance, these remnants of ancient settlements sometimes make their presence known in town names. Dr. Feinman's team found that any town with the word *dun*, meaning "platform," in its name was an excellent prospect to be the site of an ancient community and its associated artifacts.

Since Dr. Feinman began visiting China, he has witnessed dramatic growth in the

towns, roads, and railroads of Shandong. This modern hustle and bustle, however, threatens remnants of the prehistoric past. "This happens all over the world," Dr. Feinman notes, "but it's of concern here because the history is so rich and the pace of development is so fast." This trend reinforces why the regional survey is so important. "When you find a site that was completely unknown," Dr. Feinman says, "you put something on the rolls of history that had been lost. And it could have been lost forever if a highway had come along."

In a province about the size of the state of Rhode Island, Dr. Feinman's teams identified more than seven hundred archeological sites from the Longshan period, dating from 2600 to 1900 BC. By mapping quantities and locations of tools and pottery shards scattered across the land, Dr. Feinman determines the sizes of settlements and the distances between them. "Just like the roadbuilding and urbanization today," he says, "the Longshan period shows a big investment in infrastructure for the public good. In those days, it was in the form of defensive walls that ringed cities and earthen platforms where community rituals were enacted."

Dr. Feinman's research also reveals evidence for significant episodes of population growth. The Longshan lived in regional centers with more than five thousand residents, surrounded by smaller towns (much like today's cities, surrounded by suburbs). Farming was the key to feeding this many people living in one place. Through farming, some people could produce enough surplus to support others who spent barely any time acquiring food. This freed some to devote themselves to weaving, producing tools, or carving jade. Surplus also fed those who hauled tons of earth to fortify settlement walls—plus members of the elite class who coordinated such projects. Such organization of labor indicates more social stratification, which is the division of society based on status and wealth.

Sometimes entire neighborhoods or towns specialized in an occupation. At the Longshan village of Taosi, which is outside the range of Dr. Feinman's surveys, other

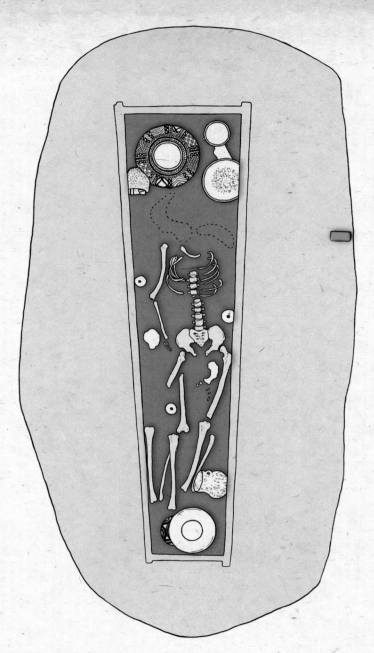

Neolithic graves often have objects for use in the afterlife. Archaeologists believe those with the most grave goods also had the highest status in life.

archaeologists have found piles of remnants from making stone tools. Nearby settlements had finished tools, without the related debris, that matched those made at Taosi. Archaeologists concluded that Taosi, which was located near a quarry, supplied tools to surrounding areas.

Controlling resources, skills, and labor were paths to building status in the ancient world, just as they are today. The distribution of artifacts at Longshan sites signals that some people had more wealth than others. In the early Neolithic period, almost everyone was buried with a few objects—maybe a ceramic jar or a stone ax. As time went on, some people began to be buried with more and fancier items. In Liangzhu society, which existed south of Longshan settlements, some gravesites held nothing but human bones, while others included more than fifty bi disks of jade. The most elaborate Liangzhu burial found was a man-made, earthen mound that held eleven graves and eleven hundred jade objects.

The wealthiest graves of Longshan communities included tall, black goblets that were likely made specifically for burial because the eggshell-like pottery is too thin to hold liquid. Goblets for the living—still delicate, but sturdy enough for use—have been found with dried traces of an alcoholic drink made from rice, honey, and fruit. Scholars believe Longshan high society honored ancestors with feasts and ceremonial drinking rituals.

Some Longshan burials included delicate goblets. The darkened section of the illustration represents an actual potsherd that survived. Archaeologists combine information from many artifacts to piece together a vision of the complete goblet.

Dr. Feinman never tires of examining pottery shards because they embody so many aspects of a culture. "A scientist doesn't just say, 'This is a pretty bowl, so it's more advanced,'" he explains. "Rather, you observe what artifacts can tell us about how things were made and how neighboring peoples may have interacted." The Longshan goblets were shaped on fast-turning potters' wheels, which hadn't been invented by earlier cultures. Making them required expertise and close attention because such fine clay could easily break in the blaze of the kiln.

Like technology, the development of human culture is somewhat cumulative, with new ideas building on old ones. Yet Dr. Feinman cautions against viewing the development of technology—and culture—as a continuous path toward constant improvement. "Archaeologists used to talk about progress," he says. "Now we talk about change." By tracking broad shifts in various societies through space and time, Dr. Feinman's team documents a picture of constant change. Neolithic societies influenced each other through trade, warfare, and migration. Customs, crops, technology, and the surrounding environment also continued to evolve.

People living in Hongshan settlements, for example, may have scattered due to famine. Patterns in the sand dunes of Liaoning Province suggest that about forty-two hundred years ago, an area of lakes and lush woodlands about the size of the state of New Jersey suddenly withered into a desert. This may have prompted people to relocate, taking Hongshan traditions to mingle with the customs of other groups and be passed down in new forms. "People seem able to change elements of identity within three or four generations," Dr. Feinman says. "That is long for a single person's lifetime, but on the scale of archaeological time, change may occur rapidly."

IMAGINE LONGSHAN VILLAGE LIFE FOUR THOUSAND YEARS AGO . . .

Your home is larger than some houses in town, but smaller than others. Anyone can see that your family is successful because you hired the extra labor to make adobe bricks for walls. The house sits on a mini-mound of dirt that rises several feet above ground level. Lots of paths intersect this large village, which is anchored around a huge central plaza.

With five thousand residents, this metropolis is so big that you can't see the edge of it from your house. You know, however, that dozens of workers are there, sweating and heaving dirt onto the massive wall that discourages bandits and warlords from raiding the city. This tiring task benefits the whole community, so almost every family takes a turn sending someone to contribute. The city's wealthiest and most powerful leaders supervise. Some here earn a living as potters, brewers of alcohol, toolmakers, and jade carvers. Your family members are accomplished weavers of fine silk. You do much of your work in the courtyard of your home, visiting with friends who pass by.

Your family trades for some of your food, which is brought into the settlement by farmers who live in smaller towns nearby. For the rest, you own a few animals and catch fish in the river. Millet and rice are your dietary staples, along with seasonal fruits and vegetables. Meat and eggs come either from your own livestock or from wild animals hunted in the surrounding forest. You regularly gather in the plaza for ceremonies and feasts to honor the ancestors and enlist their blessings of good fortune. Although your own clothing is woven from the rougher fibers of hemp and ramie plants, you take pride in seeing society's elite wear silk woven by your family. When the elite die, their families buy more silk to honor loved ones in their graves.

Neolithic pottery, c. 3400–2000 BC

Plants and animals domesticated in East Asia

POTTERY

Long ago someone must have noticed that raw clay hardens when left near fire. This likely sparked the idea of baking clay into useful shapes. The oldest-known pottery fragments were found in Jiangxi Province and date back twenty thousand years.

In early Neolithic times, people built up the walls of vessels by coiling ropes of clay and then smoothing the sides. Later potters used a fast-spinning wheel to make their work more efficient and consistent.

Neolithic peoples experimented with controlling heat in kilns they dug into the ground. They used different clays. They explored how to achieve different finishes of color and sheen, and they decorated pots with countless designs. These variations help archaeologists identify regions where people share common traditions. They also reveal patterns of trade and exchange.

DOMESTICATED PIGS

People in the past accommodated and nurtured wild animals and bred them to emphasize key traits. Over many generations, this led to new domesticated forms. So pigs, cattle, chickens, and other domesticated animals are the result of selection for specific characteristics. Based on genetic evidence, pigs were first domesticated in East Asia around 7000 BC. Multiple societies living in the Yangtze and Yellow River valleys seemed to come up with this idea independently.

By around 4500 BC, pigs had become symbols of social status. At a site near Xinglongwa, in Inner Mongolian Autonomous Region, archaeologists found the complete skeletons of a male and female pig in a human grave from that time. This practice of sacrificing pigs for a human burial became common among elites in some of China's Neolithic societies.

Oldest-known lacquered bowl

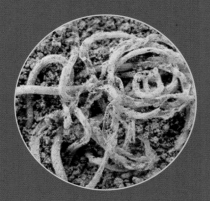

Four-thousand-year-old noodles

LACQUER

The oldest-known lacquered bowl was found at a Hemudu site, dating from about six or seven thousand years ago. Lacquer is a varnish made from the resin of the lacquer tree (*Toxicodendron verniciflluum*). Villagers collected tree resin and then carefully brushed it in thin layers on wooden bowls and tools. With multiple coats, the lacquered object became waterproof and developed a shine. With the addition of red, black, and other pigments, lacquer can be used to paint elaborate scenes. Over time, lacquer became a distinct art form, prized on everything from cups to coffins.

NOODLES

The world's oldest-known noodles were discovered beneath a bowl that tipped over in northwest China, and then was buried under ten feet of sediment that formed a stay-fresh seal for four thousand years. Based on seed husks found nearby, scientists believe the noodles were made from millet. The long, thin noodles look like the hand-stretched *lamian* noodles made in China today.

Silkworms

Top: Silkworm larvae eat for three weeks before spinning cocoons.
Bottom: It takes three thousand cocoons to make enough thread for one yard of silk fabric.

SILK

The oldest-known silk fragments were found in a forty-eight-hundred-year-old tomb in China. No one knows, however, when people figured out that the delicate cocoons of *Bombyx mori* moths could be boiled and then unraveled into delicate strands more than half a mile long. When spun together, these wispy fibers form a strong thread, which is then woven into a fabric so soft and distinct that the word *silky* is its own adjective.

Neolithic farmers tended silkworm caterpillars by feeding them fresh mulberry leaves several times a day. Making silk was time-consuming, so only the wealthy could afford to buy it.

第二章

CHAPTER TWO

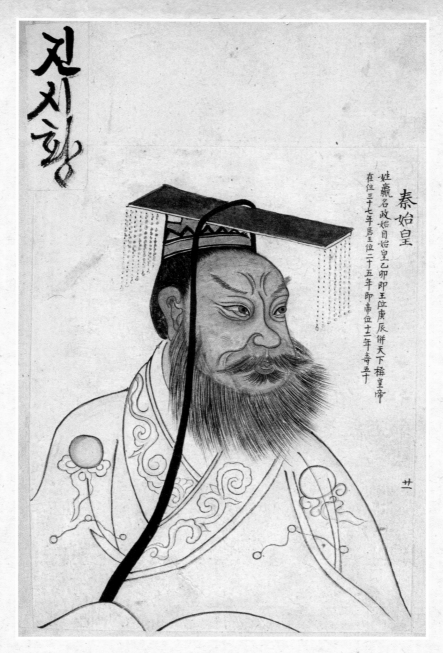

秦始皇

姓嬴名政始目始皇乙卯即王位庚辰併天下稱皇帝
在位三十七年居王位二十五年即帝位十二年壽五十

廿

Qin Shi Huangdi, China's first emperor, created systems that would be used to unify and reunify the empire for thousands of years.

王朝的出现

THE RISE OF DYNASTIES

BRONZE, IRON, PAPER, POWER

Eventually developments in metalworking ended the Neolithic period, giving rise to the Bronze Age, followed by the Iron Age. In China this occurred around 2000 BC. Manipulating bronze and iron led to stronger, sharper plows and harvesting blades . . . which spurred an agricultural boom, followed by population growth.

Increasing specialization of jobs brought more tiers in society, which in turn led to a deeper divide between the haves and the have-nots. Kings and a formal ruling class emerged. Cities were home to administrators, craftspeople, and traders. Most people, however, scraped by as peasants who farmed and provided muscle for a ruler's ambitious schemes. Criminals, prisoners of war, and those in debt sometimes became slaves.

Writings like the one above were carved in stone. Ink rubbing was then used to distribute the information widely.

Meanwhile more goods increased opportunities for trade, and more trade brought more chances for disputes. Intensified conflict, combined with abundant weapons from metalworking, led to a surge in warfare. Constant social turmoil inspired great thinkers to ponder philosophies that might restore peace. In particular, they questioned the relationship between subjects and rulers.

The Bronze and Iron Ages also witnessed a flowering of creativity that brought about such inventions as currency, writing, paper, and printing to the ancient lands of China. Communicating became easier and public works benefitted ever-growing groups of people. Educational academies began, along with a government bureaucracy and military structure that allowed for advancement based on merit.

These innovations of technology and social structures became the tools for unifying China's diverse peoples. An imperial census in AD 2 documented China to have nearly fifty-eight million residents, a third of the world's estimated population at the time. By comparison, a census of the Roman Empire in AD 14 reported five million residents. Core ideas that developed during the Bronze Age were used to govern China's vast empire for thousands of years. When leadership changed within a dynasty, which is a series of rulers from the same family, the basic style of governing remained. And each time the empire temporarily fell apart, later rulers relied on similar strategies to bring people back together.

EARLY KINGDOMS UNIFY AND DIVIDE

The Shang Dynasty is the first for which written records exist. Beginning around 1600 BC, the Shang gained power in an area that centered around the Yellow River and was about one-tenth the size of modern China.

The Shang ruled over a period of great prosperity and innovation, symbolized by its thriving bronze industry. In Egypt and Mesopotamia during this time, people hammered hot and cold metal into shapes as best they could. Meanwhile in China,

people melted metal into liquid and poured it into molds. Metalworking evolved from the expertise built up by firing pottery. Eventually kilns became hot enough to melt copper, which is mixed with tin to make bronze.

"Bronze production during this era reached an unprecedented scale," says Dr. Yung-ti Li, an archaeologist at the University of Chicago. "The Shang capital of An-yang was an epicenter of resource consumption and craft production." Metal ores from mines hundreds of miles away flowed into Anyang, where masses of workers cast them into bronze mirrors, vessels, weapons, and bells. The first step in this process was to make a full-size clay model of the final product. This model was baked, and then surrounded by more clay to make a relief of both the shape and the intricate decorations of dragons, tigers, and long-tailed birds. When fired in the kiln and then carefully separated into sections, this outer layer became a mold. Another team of craftsmen poured melted bronze into finished molds. "The foundries needed

Left: Metalworking introduced new status symbols, like this bronze wine vessel made more than twenty-two hundred years ago.
Right: Thirty-six hundred years ago, bronze became the preferred choice for weapons because it is tough and pliable and it can take a sharp edge.

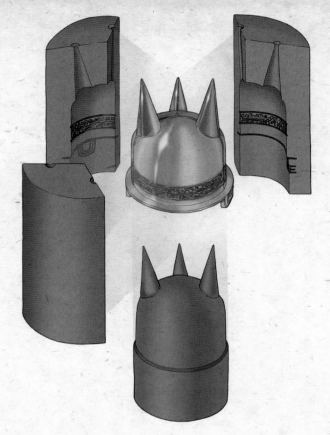

Liquid bronze was poured into molds made of baked clay. Here
four molds fit together to form the shape of a wine vessel (*center*).

specialists in ceramics and metal, plus sophisticated management to coordinate the
work," Dr. Li says. "This was large-scale production taking place in the ancient world."

Researchers estimate that a single eighteen-hundred-pound ceremonial vessel
required the efforts of two to three hundred workers. As a result, many people's en-
ergies went into creating items that only an elite few could afford. Graves of Bronze
Age nobles have been found with more than ten tons of bronze objects—along with
the bodies of prisoner-of-war slaves whose lives in this world were sacrificed to serve
rulers in the next.

Music accompanied many court rituals. These bronze bells, the most complete set ever discovered, were found in a royal tomb from 433 BC.

Over time, the decadence of Shang kings wore out its welcome among their subjects. Around 1046 BC, the Zhou Dynasty wrested control, claiming to have the Mandate of Heaven. Through this principle, gods rewarded virtuous rulers with success and flawed rulers with famine, war, and defeat. The legendary telling of the Zhou victory supports this idea: Only heaven's blessing could explain why forty-eight thousand Zhou troops defeated seven hundred thousand Shang troops. From then on, each new dynasty justified its rise to power as a supernatural reprimand for unworthy rulers. Those who held the throne called themselves the Sons of Heaven.

Charioteers would have used this bronze blade atop a long pole to sweep opponents away.

Guidance from the gods was crucial for dynastic rulers. Would they support attacking another state? Would the hunt succeed? Would a toothache never end? Shang and Zhou kings sought answers from oracle bones. Cattle bones and turtle plastrons (the hard belly shields) were polished and prodded with hot pokers. When these items cracked, the popping noises were considered the voices of ancestors. Diviners carved questions into the bones, interpreted the cracks, and then etched the answers from the gods. Later, the accuracy of predictions was also recorded. Since 1900 more than two hundred thousand oracle bones have been discovered, providing the first known examples of writing in China. Many characters—this language uses a unique symbol for each word—in modern Chinese writing can be traced back to marks made on oracle bones.

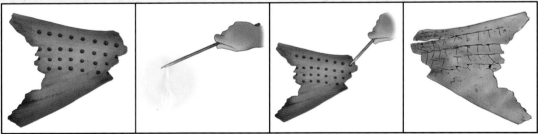

Top: Shang Dynasty oracle bones.
Bottom: Pits were bored into polished cow bones or turtle plastrons. A heated metal rod was poked into the pits. The cracking of the bones represented ancestors speaking. Diviners analyzed the shapes of the cracks, hoping for news of the future.

Cowrie shells, which were rare and valuable inland, served as currency for the Shang Dynasty. The numbers show these artifacts have been catalogued in a museum collection.

Everyday life under Shang and Zhou rule was mostly the same. Trading became so widespread and frequent that the Shang used seashells from the cowrie snail as currency, and the Zhou introduced the world's first coins. Beginning during the Zhou Dynasty, peasants in the countryside lived on feudal estates, working the lands of local lords to whom they owed crops, game, and weavings. In return, the lords provided clothing, feasts, and protection. Higher up, kings gave the local lords their land rights and social status—taking in return a share of the wealth produced, along with tenants to serve as soldiers.

By the Zhou period, a system of quality control was at work in the bronze industry. Inscriptions on the works themselves named artisans responsible for different phases of manufacturing, plus state officials who oversaw the process. Meanwhile cast-iron manufacturing took off. "Bronze was the metal for the elite," Dr. Li explains, "but iron became the metal for the masses, being widely used to make utilitarian tools and weapons."

Arming troops became less expensive and warfare changed dramatically. At

first, nobles charged into battle in chariots pulled by four galloping horses. Chariots, however, made for large targets and often broke or sank into muddy terrain. Nobles grumbled when generals ordered them to run alongside the rank and file. They groused even more when rulers began promoting within military ranks based on performance rather than birthright.

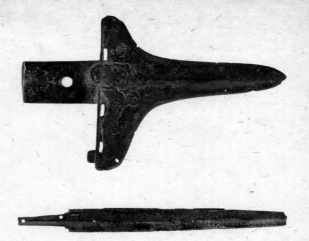

Zhou Dynasty halberd and sword blades. As armies used fewer war chariots, foot soldiers preferred swords, rather than battle-axes, for hand-to-hand combat.

As the abundance of weapons and military expertise grew, so did threats to Zhou authority. In the eighth century BC, central China was home to more than one hundred states. Some of these were the size of a modern European nation; others were just one walled city. The Zhou ruling class suffered constant challenges, and for some years, the dynasty's control beyond its capital was in name only. From 722 to 463 BC—a period of just over two hundred fifty years—one ancient historian reported more than five hundred battles between states and more than one hundred civil wars within states. This trend continued, and the years from 475 to 221 BC are known as the Warring States period.

These centuries also spurred what scholars call the Hundred Schools of Thought. Constant violence inspired wise sages to reflect on the roles of individuals in society and to clarify rules for ethical behavior. Around 500 BC, Confucius began encouraging people to treat each other with mutual respect. At the same time Lao-tzu, the legendary founder of Taoism, urged a life of simplicity and harmony with nature. Although famous now, in their own time these were just two voices among many. A sage named Mozi advised people to consider their obligations

The cap and three-part beard identify Lao-tzu, who began as one of many voices among the Hundred Schools of Thought.

to all fellow humans, not just family and rulers. A scholar named Xunzi believed rigorous education and devotion to ritual would balance the weaknesses in human nature. The list of thinkers and their ideas could go on. Most of these wise men sought to influence the decisions of royal courts. All hoped their teachings would bring peace and stability. Such philosophies of compassion would profoundly influence Chinese culture.

As the scale and complexity of settlements expanded in the Bronze and Iron Ages, people around the world needed new strategies for living together—spurring what remain widespread religions in the world today. Judaism began around 2000 BC, followed by Hinduism around 1500 BC. The birth of Christ marks what Western nations call the Common Era for counting years, providing the dividing line between years that are labeled BC and AD. Islam originated around AD 600.

EMPERORS SET THE COURSE OF HISTORY

Eventually through either alliance or conquest, the groups of central China evolved into seven large states centered between the Yellow and Yangtze rivers. Among these, the Qin state came to dominate. Following the advice of shrewd ministers, Qin leaders repealed land rights from feudal lords and divided land among those who worked it. Then every subject owed allegiance directly to the king, who set high standards for subjects to deliver grain and cloth, perform military service, and contribute to public works. Qin ministers also developed management techniques to hold bureaucrats accountable, making government more efficient and effective. Basically, everyone in Qin society had to prove their worth as a producer and everyone had to follow orders. A thinker named Han Fei consolidated the ideas of others with his own in a book that outlined a philosophy called Legalism. In this way of thinking, a state could only succeed through strict laws, reinforced with a fair system of rewards and punishments.

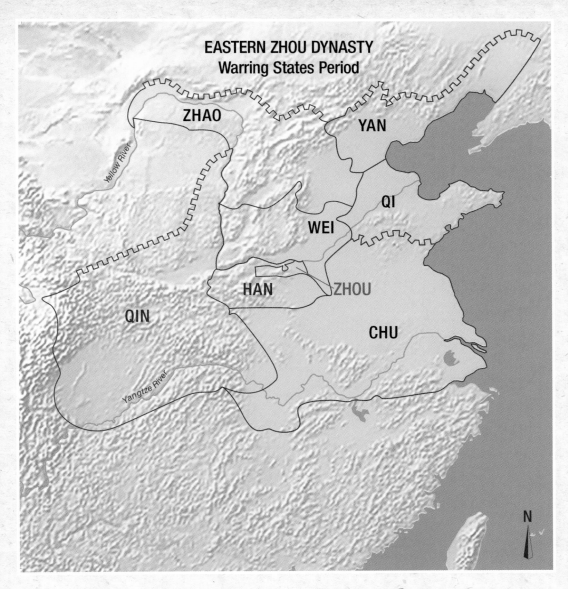

EASTERN ZHOU DYNASTY
Warring States Period

At the start of the Warring States period, dozens of states occupied this region. After two hundred years of constant conflict, these seven states surrounding the seat of the Zhou Dynasty were all that remained.

Qin Shi Huangdi invented a new title to declare his authority over previous kings. *Shi* means "start," as in the beginning of a dynasty. *Huangdi,* which usually translates as "emperor," more literally means "august lord."

Han Fei's writings greatly influenced the Qin king, who in 221 BC unified an area that was about one-third the size of modern China. To signal his victory and solidify his authority, the king gave himself a new title: Shi Huangdi, which is usually translated as "first emperor." When Qin Shi Huangdi carved his story into stone, he announced, "Now today the Emperor has unified all under heaven under one lineage. Warfare will not arise again!" The first emperor distributed copies of his edicts—inscribed on stone, bronze, pottery, and bamboo—throughout the realm to proclaim his glory.

Qin Shi Huangdi erected stone tablets that trumpeted his glory. Ink rubbings like the one above preserved the inscriptions, even as the monuments eroded over time.

The first emperor of Qin applied his systematic ruling methods to the new empire, eliminating feudal estates and dividing the land into more than forty commanderies, each subdivided into smaller counties. Within these regions, he appointed imperial officials to collect taxes and enforce laws. He also confiscated existing currencies, issued new coins, made weights and measures uniform, and identified standard widths for roads and cart axles.

Using character-based writing was a great advantage in unifying varied groups. When Qin Shi Huangdi decreed that writing be standardized throughout the empire, subjects could write in Chinese characters to communicate, even if unable to speak to one another. Consider how the modern world uses such numerals as 1, 2, and 3.

To make trade and collecting taxes easier, Qin Shi Huangdi standardized measures, weights, and currency. These two official vessels were used for measuring grain by volume.

The meanings of these symbols are recognized worldwide, although people call the numbers by different names. This helps explain why the Chinese language today has hundreds of varieties. Some of these are separate, unrelated languages in which speakers cannot understand one another. Others are dialects, which are variations of the same language. All these spoken traditions exist alongside a shared writing system, some elements of which have survived three thousand years.

Left: The shape of the Qin coin, a circle with a square hole in the middle, was used for almost two thousand years. *Right:* A standard Qin unit of weight to be used on a scale.

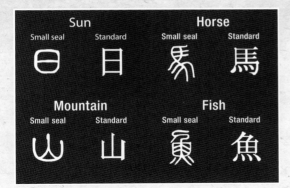

Qin Shi Huangdi used small seal script, named after the stamps once used to seal documents, to give the empire a shared written language. Its influence is evident in the standard script used today.

Public works connected the empire geographically and brought its people together around common goals. The corvée system required every family to give the emperor a certain amount of labor each year—enough to collectively build more than four thousand miles of roads. Around three hundred thousand workers also connected a series of border defenses into the Great Wall of China. The finished barricade, at three thousand miles long,

Corvée workers built dikes along the Yellow River.

slowed attacks from northern nomadic peoples. Qin Shi Huangdi also commanded armies of workers to make thousands of terracotta warrior statues to guard his eventual tomb. This monumental organization of skilled and unskilled labor relied on management techniques previously developed in bronze workshops.

Unfortunately, Legalist laws were unyielding. Those who committed crimes could lose their property and become slaves of the state—along with their families and any neighbors who did not report the crime. Thieves had their noses cut off and were sentenced to hard labor. Historical reports say the first emperor also relocated thirty thousand families to the coast just to ensure the reach of his rule. The scattering of pottery shards found by Dr. Feinman during his archaeological surveys in eastern Shandong Province provides evidence to confirm this forced migration.

Emperors required both taxes and unpaid labor from subjects. Corvée workers connected smaller defenses to create China's Great Wall, which today reflects centuries of expansions and repairs.

These massive earthen features are the remnants of a rammed earth platform likely built for Qin Dynasty rituals.

When Qin Shi Huangdi died in 210 BC, his successors were weak, and a peasant revolt ended the Qin Dynasty in 206 BC. The rebel leader, Liu Bang, was one of only two emperors in Chinese history born as a commoner. Shortly after his victory, he declared to his subjects: "You have long suffered under the harsh laws of Qin . . . My sole object in coming here is to eradicate wrong. I desire to do violence to no one." Thus began Han rule. Lasting more than four hundred years, this would become China's longest imperial dynasty. Ever since, any rulers not of the Han ethnicity—such as later Mongol and Manchu Dynasties—were considered foreign rulers. The Han are the largest ethnic group in China today.

Han emperors reduced taxes, lowered corvée requirements, and promoted

武皇帝劉秀

Emperor Wu, of the Han Dynasty, greatly expanded China's borders through military victories.

Confucian ideals of kindness and respect. They also expanded the systematic bureaucracy begun by the Qin. To fill posts, Han emperors called for recommendations from every region. A proclamation in the second century BC from Emperor Wu said, "Exceptional work demands exceptional men . . . We therefore command the various district officials to search for men of brilliant and exceptional talents, to be our generals, our ministers, and our envoys to distant states."

In addition to building roads, canals, and dams, the Han used corvée workers to mine iron ore and boil brine from underground springs to produce salt. Han emperors took over these industries and funneled their profits into the treasury. Some court scholars argued against these government monopolies, wanting the emperor to encourage traditional lifestyles in which people produced most of what they needed for themselves. These same officials argued that the government should discourage merchant trading because they believed that

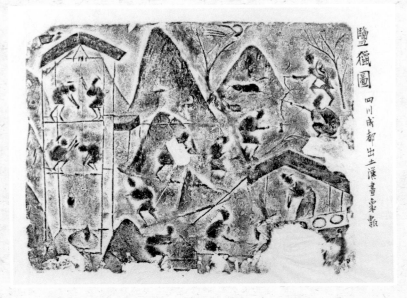

This rubbing shows Han Dynasty salt production. Men hoist salty water from an underground spring and then a pipeline carries the brine to basins where the water boils away.

making money from goods produced by others promoted dishonesty. Economic ministers disagreed, championing monopolies because their profits reduced taxes for citizens and trade because items common in China were uncommon elsewhere. "A piece of Chinese plain silk," one Han Dynasty minister explained, "can be exchanged with the Xiongnu for articles worth several pieces of gold and thereby reduce the resources of our enemy . . . That is to say, foreign products keep flowing in, while our wealth is not dissipated."

The Xiongnu were a group of nomadic tribes north of the Great Wall who took turns being invaders and trading partners. In the second century BC, the Han emperor worried that the Xiongnu would attack, so he sent a diplomatic envoy named Zhang Qian in search of allies. While exploring states west

Two men pump bellows, which blow air into the furnace. This makes the fire hot enough to melt iron, which pours out of the spout. Han rulers built blast furnaces across the empire.

of China's border, Zhang Qian noticed that Chinese goods the Xiongnu had acquired had then been traded much farther. This discovery led to centuries of profitable trading over what would become known as the Silk Road. This collection of travel routes stretched more than four thousand six hundred miles from northeastern China to the Mediterranean Sea.

Many things contributed to the fall of the Han Dynasty. Deadly floods and crop-gobbling locusts besieged the countryside, and peasants revolted when the

government couldn't keep up with relief. Reduced taxes did not help the treasury, which was already straining to support a vast territory. Meanwhile, inside the court, those who managed day-to-day affairs hatched plots and intrigue.

After the Han Dynasty ended in AD 220, the empire endured four hundred years of weak states. Short-lived dynasties controlled diminished territories for brief periods of time. Nevertheless the tools for unification had been established. Each time the empire broke apart, a new dynasty would rise again. Finally, the Tang Dynasty, beginning in AD 618, brought several centuries of stability.

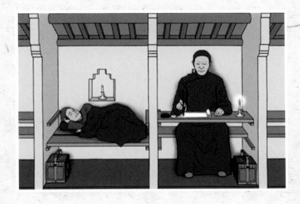

Takers of civil service tests rearranged boards to serve as beds and desks.

THE PRESSURES OF LIFE IN THE COURT

Shouldering the Mandate of Heaven was daunting. China's emperors were responsible for the welfare of their subjects and for maintaining harmony between the human and spirit worlds. If the empire thrived, it was because the ruler had secured supernatural favor. If people suffered, then they could assume the gods had revoked support from a cruel or inept ruler—so deposing him had heavenly approval. Such action usually meant the start of a new dynasty.

This gave emperors strong incentive to create effective governments. The bureaucracy that began in the Qin Dynasty strengthened a ruler's position by attracting educated officials who owed the emperor loyalty for their careers. In 124 BC the Han Dynasty established the first government-sponsored academy to prepare those seeking imperial jobs. The school began with fifty students, but grew to three thousand students within its first seventy-five years.

The Han administration identified the classics of Confucianism as the primary course of study. Centuries later, in the nineteenth-century Qing court, these remained important subjects. To sit for their exams, Qing applicants took up residence for three stressful days and two sleepless nights in rooms about the size of a small closet. They carried in only food and a small basket of writing implements. To prevent cheating, guards frisked students from head to toe and even checked inside dumplings. Still, scholars smuggled in notes, some by sewing silken cheat sheets into the linings of their robes.

Top: Scholars spent three days in these tiny cells.
Bottom: Imperial governments needed thousands of officials—and so thousands of examination cells.

This silk cheat sheet contains texts that aspiring scholars were supposed to memorize. Guards patrolled examination compounds to prevent cheating.

Scholars were also patrons of the arts, including calligraphy, painting, and poetry. Calligraphy is an art of writing that celebrates the graceful formation of characters. It took years to master and set scholar-officials apart from merchants and farmers who could write as a practical skill but not as an art form. Painting encouraged scholars to reflect on nature and connections between past and present because they often reinterpreted classic masterpieces. Poetry challenged scholars to communicate with precision. A common form of Chinese art combines these skills—with a poem inscribed in calligraphy onto a painting—to present viewers with an inspiring combination of images and words.

In theory, the civil service examination was open to all. In reality, few commoners could afford the years of study required to pass the examinations and secure a position. Plus, despite the ideals of the system, politics frequently came into play. In some courts, great pains were taken to grade exams anonymously, while in other courts, graders knew exactly whose papers they reviewed. Over time the civil service bureaucracy developed a new class of citizens. The years of study, followed by government service, gave scholar-officials a set of life experiences and perspectives that was distinct from other groups.

Emperors were expected to cultivate an interest in the arts. This Qing emperor contemplates calligraphy.

ROLE OF WOMEN IN COURT LIFE

Women played a unique role in court life. Although there could only be one empress, a ruler could have many wives and concubines (women who belonged to a household but did not have the same rights as wives). Men at every level of society who could afford to do so took on concubines as a strategy for having more sons. In a royal court, the ruler's wives and concubines, plus their attendants, could number in the thousands. A ranking system determined each woman's specific duties—preparing food, weaving, managing living quarters, providing music, performing religious rites, and many other tasks needed for the court to run smoothly.

Although the official governing bureaucracy did not invite women into state affairs, those who had the ear of the emperor also had influence. Wives, mothers, and sisters of the ruler had the most social status; throughout China's history some women wielded enough power to attract the attention of historians. In the Shang Dynasty, a consort of ruler Wu Ding (c. 1250–1192 BC) named Lady Hao led armies

Women of the Tang Dynasty court wore richly dyed gowns, as shown in this scroll, circa eighth century AD.

Lady Hao was a powerful woman and military leader during the Shang Dynasty. This modern statue stands near her tomb, discovered in 1976.

Clothes communicated every person's rank at court. Embroidered badges signal the status of this official and his family.

into battle and owned a landed estate. Her prominence was reflected in her grave, which included more than five hundred jade objects, nearly seven thousand cowrie shells, twenty-three bronze bells, and hundreds more bronze ritual vessels, weapons, and mirrors. Later when the first Han emperor died, Empress Lu ensured the stability and continuance of the young dynasty. Unfortunately, historians also suspect her of murdering four young princes who held claims to the throne.

Eunuchs were another influential group within the court. Because they had been castrated and could not father children, eunuchs were the only men (besides the emperor) allowed in the women's quarters. Consequently, eunuchs ran day-to-day court affairs and were often counted among an emperor's most trusted advisers. For eunuchs, joining the court was often a choice between the extremes of starving poverty and a life of unimaginable luxury. It was thought eunuchs would not covet power, but that was not always the case.

Natural disasters, corrupt officials and advisers, and waging war could chip away at an emperor's strength. So could misjudging what subjects would bear in terms of taxes or demands to fight battles and build roads. Sometimes emperors became drunk on their own power, ignoring subjects' needs or acting cruelly—forgetting that the blessings of the gods also came with responsibilities.

Time and time again, such mistakes put dynasties in danger. Sometimes another powerful group or neighboring state launched a dramatic takeover. Other times a centralized authority fizzled into centuries of war before anyone amassed the power to assume the title of emperor again.

LIFE OUTSIDE THE COURT

For most of Chinese history, farmers remained the backbone of society. With the invention of cast-iron tools in the Zhou period, farmers produced a lot more food

Cast-iron tools, like this twenty-two-hundred-year-old axe, made farming easier because they were sharper and stronger than stone or bronze.

with their efforts. Iron axes made clearing trees from fields easier. Iron plows dug up soils that had previously been too stubborn to till. Iron sickles sliced stalks efficiently at harvest. Besides grain, farmers gave feudal lords livestock, game, and labor. After the feudal system was eliminated, farmers paid taxes directly to emperors in the form of money, grain, labor, and military service.

An ancient song describes common activities of winter:

In the days of the First [month] we hunt the raccoon,
And take those foxes and wild-cats
To make furs for our Lord.
In the days of the Second is the great Meet;
Practice for deeds of war.
The one-year-old [boar] we keep;
The three-year-old we offer to our Lord.

Farmers worried as much about floods as they did about drought. Farming speeds up soil erosion, letting rains in central China wash silt into the Yellow River. Over time, silt builds up, raising the riverbed. Rulers were constantly building levees to keep

floods in check, but if one burst, all could be lost. In the first century AD, a flood displaced millions of people. Masses of silt sealed the farmstead of Sanyangzhuang in a time capsule that was discovered in 2003.

For archaeologists, Sanyangzhuang provides a wealth of information about daily farming life two thousand years ago. Families lived in walled compounds with buildings that opened onto interior courtyards. Houses had walls of packed earth and were roofed by ceramic tiles with decorations and sayings like "Long life without end!" Farmers placed pigpens and latrines downwind. Wells for drinking, cooking, and washing were at opposite corners of the family compound. Successful farmers produced what was needed to feed and clothe their families, as well as pay taxes. A farmer with extra to sell to traders was very successful indeed.

During the Qin Dynasty, Legalists declared merchants to be the least contributing members of society because, unlike farmers, they did not produce the goods they sold themselves. This view stuck for

Sanyangzhuang is called the "Chinese Pompeii" because thick layers of fine silt preserved details of daily life.
Top: Impressions of mulberry leaves are clues that residents made silk.
Bottom: An excavation reveals how layers of silt left behind from Yellow River floods built up over thousands of years.

centuries, despite the obvious need for this occupation. As the philosopher Xunzi once pointed out, the central states relied on imported goods:

> In the far north there are fast horses and howling dogs . . . In the far south there are feathers, tusks, hides, pure copper, and cinnabar . . . in the far east there are plants with purple dye, coarse hemp, fish, and salt . . . In the far west there are skins and colored yaks' tails; the central states acquire them [all] for their needs.

Perhaps rulers took a dim view of traders because they saw their growing wealth as a threat. They also worried that traders might serve as spies, selling to foreigners secrets from the imperial court or China's most profitable industries.

Decorated roof tiles were found during the excavation of Sanyangzhuang, left behind when the inhabitants fled the coming flood. The characters on these roof tiles read "longevity."

For centuries markets were heavily regulated, as illustrated by those from the seventh-century Tang Dynasty. In the capital of Chang'an (now Xi'an), markets opened for business at noon and closed at sundown. They sold everything from locally produced silks, grain, and iron tools to items from afar, such as pepper, silver, and ivory. State-appointed market directors checked weights and measures, inspected the quality of goods, and set prices for each commodity. They also issued certificates of ownership to document sales of slaves, livestock, and land.

The Tang markets thrived. Although the state minted more than one million strings of bronze coins annually, there often were not enough coins in circulation to serve all the business being transacted. Bolts of cloth, particularly silk, also served as currency.

The Tang capital of Chang'an, shown here in a scale model, reached two million residents. Today the city is called Xi'an, with a population of more than eight million.

Emperor Taizong wrote the Tang Code, a new set of laws that influenced all later dynasties, plus Korean and Japanese legal systems.

Continued prosperity eventually led to a commercial revolution, beginning around AD 1000. Under the Song Dynasty, merchants moved beyond designated market zones to set up shop on any street. Markets also expanded into the countryside, where farmers began taking a more direct role in selling their own commodities.

Throughout Chinese history, the fortunes of most women were bound up in decisions made by men. When young, girls were taught to put the desires of fathers and brothers before their own. When grown, women were expected to follow husbands' directions. When elderly, widows were to be guided by sons. These teachings were supported by tradition, plus the codes of Confucianism, Taoism, and Buddhism. Although beloved, daughters were underappreciated from birth because they would eventually leave to join their husbands' families after marriage. A legendary quote from a woman wanting to become a Buddhist nun in the fourth century articulates her frustration with this situation: "Why must I submit thrice to father, husband, and son," she asked, "before I am considered a woman of propriety?"

Social status also defined women's lives. Poor peasant women worked constantly: cooking, caring for children, weaving cloth, and walking for hours to turn human-powered waterwheels that irrigated crops. In the upper classes, women had opportunity for education and leisure but less freedom outside the home. They spent most of their lives in an inner sanctum, sending servants to complete any business in public. Within this realm, however, many women had significant personal authority—being expected to manage the buildings, staff, and stores of complex households. Some were deeply involved in family businesses, although their contributions were credited to men in their families. In rare cases women became well known for their work. Exceptions include Ban Zhao, a respected historian during the Han Dynasty, and twelfth-century Li Qingzhao, one of China's most famous poets.

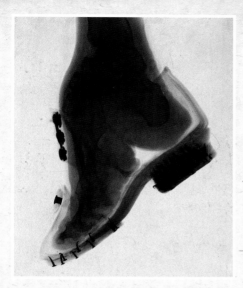

One custom that restricted women in Chinese society was foot-binding, which probably emerged during the Song Dynasty in the tenth century AD. Concubines who wrapped their feet for dancing may have inspired foot-binding. The practice spread among wealthier classes, especially those who were ethnically Han. In rural areas, mothers began wrapping daughters' feet before their bones matured in the hopes that such perceived daintiness would bring upward social mobility. Foot-binding began when girls were four to seven years old. Over time the feet would become permanently misshapen and need the support of the bindings for the rest of a woman's life. If the process went well, a woman could walk short distances without pain. If not, any standing or stepping would hurt. This practice continued for centuries. In the nineteenth century, 50 percent of all Chinese women and almost all upper-class women had bound feet.

The bottom photograph shows how women looked with their feet bound. It was often hard for these women to walk without pain. This X-ray (*top*) from the 1920s shows how foot-binding had deformed the foot of a forty-three-year-old woman. Foot-binding was officially banned in 1911.

An exhausted scholar dreams of success.

Farming could be an unpredictable livelihood.

IMAGINE BEING A SCHOLAR-OFFICIAL . . .

Although most imperial subjects cannot read, you have been lucky enough to study history, literature, and the arts. You'll be even luckier if you pass your civil service exams with high marks. To do so, you must write eloquent essays, compose lyrical poems, re-create passages of the classics from memory, and write thousands of classical Chinese characters.

You dream of rising through government ranks to attract the emperor's favor. Everyone would notice if he honors you with a peacock feather to tuck into your cap. More likely, you will never meet the emperor, as you are assigned to a series of posts in the provinces. There you will maintain order, report on local events, and be a role model of refinement through your speech, your manners, and your possessions.

IMAGINE BEING A FARMER IN ANCIENT CHINA . . .

Men in your family toil for long hours cultivating fields and livestock. And every man of a certain age takes turns reporting for corvée duty to build bridges, forge iron, or serve in the infantry. Meanwhile women cook, weave, and often labor in the fields as well.

A well is your best defense against drought and the famine that often follows it. The second best is being able to store extra grain from year to year. Hopefully you won't need either backup plan because the village held a feast asking cloud gods to bring rain and not locusts. Whatever happens, you'll need enough grain when taxes come due. Otherwise you might have to borrow money that you'll later repay at twice the price. Or if things get really bad, your family might have to sell land or even children. That will only make taxes harder to pay in the future.

Merchants often used camels along the Silk Road.

Children sometimes wore patchwork robes, similar to those of monks, to show humility and attract blessings.

IMAGINE BEING A MERCHANT IN AN ANCIENT CAPITAL . . .

Traditional Chinese society looks down on you because your family buys and sells what others produce. Plenty of peasants, however, would gladly swap their lives for yours.

You live in the empire's capital, where interesting people are around every corner. Foreigners live nearest the markets, and Buddhist temples throughout the city offer services like hostels and public baths. The city is laid out as a grid, with gated walls surrounding each quarter and a larger wall surrounding the whole. When the drums ring out curfew, all gates are locked until sunrise.

Your family would prefer the government to stay out of trading and let you set your own prices. Nonetheless you like having a strong ruler. Peace and stability bring well-maintained, safe roads, which means more access to goods and a booming business for you.

IMAGINE BEING A CHILD IN ANCIENT CHINA . . .

Congratulations on surviving childhood so far! Infants die so often in ancient China that your family did not officially name you until you had lived for one hundred days.

If you are a girl, a book from the Han Dynasty advises your parents to place you on the floor with a pottery shard for a toy, so that you get used to the idea that your life will be full of work.

If you are a boy, you are celebrated and dressed in special clothing. Embroidered tiger slippers will hopefully lend you a tiger's strength and spirit. Or you might wear a hat with dog ears to trick evil spirits into thinking that you are not important enough to bother.

China's kilns produced many styles of porcelain to sell at home and abroad.

Ink rubbings from carved tablets were the first form of printing.

PORCELAIN

By the first century AD, during the Han Dynasty, Chinese potters could crank up the heat in kilns to twenty-four hundred degrees Fahrenheit. At this temperature they fired fine, white clay called kaolin into a ceramic called porcelain, which is highly valued for being both durable and delicate. For centuries porcelain was highly sought after in trade, and China was the only place it was produced.

PRINTING

The Chinese invented printing—twice. More than two thousand years ago, they carved words into stone tablets and then made ink rubbings of those tablets to distribute Confucian teachings and imperial proclamations. This was faster than making copies by hand, but a single mistake would ruin the whole stone. Wood was easier to carve. The earliest known, complete book printed from wood blocks is the Diamond Sutra, a scroll of more than sixteen feet that was printed from seven wood blocks in AD 868. Around AD 1040, someone carved individual characters into small blocks of clay that could be rearranged and reused to lay out different texts. Printing using moveable type wasn't invented in Europe for another four hundred years.

Qin imperial records on bamboo strips

PAPER

Before paper, Chinese clerics and scholars wrote on thin strips of wood and bamboo. Tied together, these strips rolled up into bulky books. Traditional histories say paper was invented around AD 105 by a court official, but recent archaeological discoveries suggest it appeared in northwestern China about two hundred years earlier. The paper was made by mashing hemp, tree bark, bamboo, and other plant fibers with water and then drying the pulp in thin sheets.

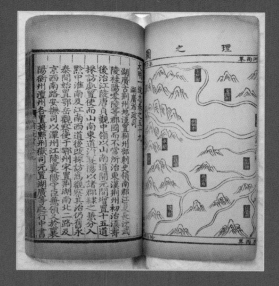

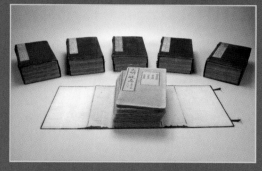

This gazetteer (*top*) is just one piece of a larger project (*below*). Gazetteers have a long history in China, possibly dating back as far as the Song Dynasty (AD 960–1279). They describe local regions in detail and can take over a decade to compile and publish. They often illustrate the geography, history, major buildings, and local customs of their region. Magistrates might order different versions that explained the regional geography, which included mountains, caves, and rivers. Others were financed by monasteries and written by Buddhist monks.

This stinkpot was filled with gunpowder, nails, metal balls, and materials that would reek when ignited.

Eighteenth-century kites

GUNPOWDER

Alchemists seeking a potion for immortality once got an explosive result. In the ninth century AD, a manual warns: "Some have heated together the saltpeter, sulfur, and carbon of charcoal with honey; smoke and flames result, so that their hands and faces have been burnt, and even the whole house burnt down." This discovery was first used for fireworks; then emperors realized its potential in battle. For a while, gunpowder warded off invasions from Mongols—until they got the secret, too, and used it against the Chinese.

KITES

As early as the fifth century BC, the Chinese experimented with kites made of wood and bamboo to send signals for military purposes. These flying machines really soared in the seventh century AD when people began making them of silk and paper. Suddenly kites became an expression of artistry and a delightful way to pass the time.

An iron stove model, made for a wealthy tomb

Coins, shaped like spades and knives, issued during the Warring States period

CAST IRON

Dating back to the Shang period, people heated iron meteorites that had been found on the ground and hammered the glowing metal into dagger blades. By 500 BC, Chinese metalworkers had invented blast furnaces, which used bellows to raise heat to twenty-eight hundred degrees Fahrenheit. This changed everything.

Iron-rich ore—rock with bits of iron mixed into it—could now be mined from underground sources in large quantities. Furnace temperatures were high enough to melt the iron into a liquid that flowed off the solid rock. The pure iron would later be melted again, mixed with other elements, and poured into molds for pots, axes, and swords. Cast iron offered more durability, precision, and affordability than previous materials. More than a thousand years would pass before such technology would become widespread in Europe.

COINS

For much of human history, people exchanged goods by bartering. Direct exchange got complicated, however, when one trader didn't need what another was offering. Besides, carrying around bolts of cloth or bundles of rice was inconvenient.

About three thousand years ago, Zhou rulers made trade easier by introducing coins. An ancient coin's value, which was sometimes stamped on its face, often related to the copper or bronze it was made of.

Some of the first metal coins were shaped like spades and knives—possibly because these were common items for bartering. People threaded spade coins onto strings through holes in the shovel handles. The Qin Dynasty later issued round coins with square holes cut in the middle, and this basic shape endured for almost two thousand years, longer than any other type of Chinese coin.

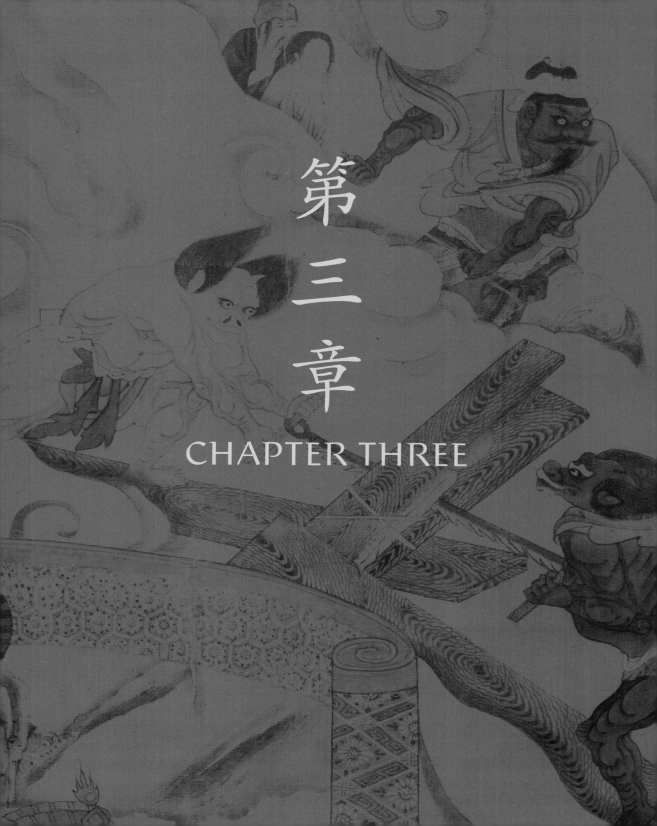

第三章

CHAPTER THREE

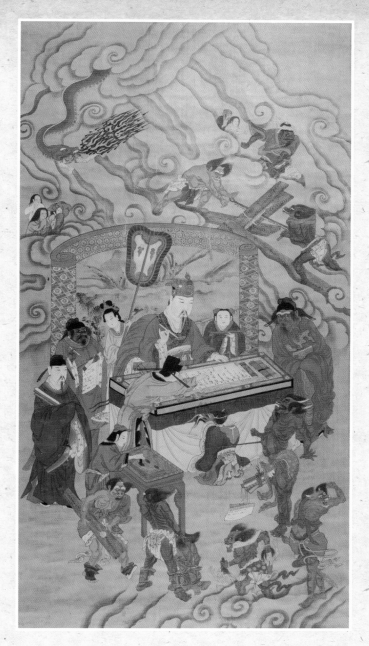

An underworld magistrate (*seated, center*) holds the dead liable for their actions in life. This vision of the underworld combines Buddhist and popular Chinese beliefs.

百家争鸣

SCHOOLS OF THOUGHT

BLENDING BELIEFS AND UNIFYING IDENTITY

Three major belief systems have had the biggest impact on Chinese culture. Confucianism originated in China about twenty-five hundred years ago, offering a philosophy about how people should treat one another. Taoism started around the same time and developed into a religion by offering spiritual guidance about both this world and the next. Buddhism, one of the world's largest religions, traveled to China over the Silk Road beginning around the first century AD.

Western and Eastern faiths promote many of the same basic morals. A key difference is that most Western religions require devotion to a single, all-powerful God, while Eastern belief systems do not. Taoism and Buddhism have dozens of deities,

each with a unique personality and sphere of influence. By contrast, Confucianism acknowledges the importance of a spiritual life, while focusing its teachings on earthly living. This flexibility allows people to blend all three doctrines, plus even older traditions of honoring ancestors and deities from local folk religions.

Although often supported by dynastic rulers, the popularity of these belief systems has ebbed and flowed depending on political priorities. They particularly suf-

Top: The teachings of Confucius explained an individual's place in society and a ruler's responsibility to his people. *Bottom*: This poster shows Buddhist figures alongside Taoist deities, illustrating how people blended elements from Eastern faiths together.

fered whenever rulers grew jealous of their influence and the wealth that sometimes grew from donations made by the devout. Yet despite the changing winds of history, the human desire for perspective on life's ups and downs is eternal. These schools of thought have been woven into the fabric of life so tightly that their teachings and stories are inseparable from Chinese identity.

CONFUCIANISM EMPHASIZES ORDER

Confucius was born in 551 BC, when Zhou rule was waning and common people suffered from local lords' constant squabbling for power. The famous sage's real name is Kong Fuzi, meaning Master Kong, but he is best known in the Western world by the Latinized name later used by Christian missionaries.

Confucius's father died when his son was young, and the boy made his way through life as a stable hand and by keeping accounts in a granary. As he grew, Confucius studied philosophy, poetry, history, and arithmetic—along with people's troubles and triumphs. He also visited the capital city to observe ancient rituals and manners.

Confucius grew up believing in the potential of all individuals to improve themselves through education and personal effort. He also believed the path to a peaceful and prosperous civilization came from people understanding how they fit into society and treating others with proper respect. Just as many Westerners know the Golden Rule from the Bible, many people from the East know this celebrated quote from Confucius: "Never impose on others what you would not choose for yourself."

Confucius identified five paired relationships as the foundation of society: father and son, husband and wife, elder brother and younger brother, friend and friend, ruler and subject. In addition, everyone had a role to play in the world, whether it was as a mighty king or a humble farmer. Confucius proposed that society succeeds when all individuals play their parts to the best of their abilities. "To put the world in

order," he said, "the ancients first put the nation in order; to put the nation in order, they put the family in order; to put the family in order, they cultivate their personal lives; and to cultivate their personal lives, they first set their hearts right."

Confucius believed his role was to save the chaotic world by reminding people of ancient customs for showing respect, including everything from the etiquette of conversation to ceremonies that honor ancestors. It worked at least once. When Confucius served as a mediator between two states that had been fighting for nine years, a group of warriors showed up unexpectedly. One duke had planned to kidnap his rival during the peace negotiation. Confucius challenged the untrustworthy leader to preserve his good name by honoring his promise to meet in friendship— and the agreement went forward.

Unfortunately Confucius found rulers of his day to be more interested in intrigue and governing by self-interest than in fulfilling obligations to their subjects. He wandered for thirteen years with a group of his followers, hoping to find a court that would promote his ideas. He died at age seventy-three, feeling like a failure for having served only a few years in any government. Most of his career had been spent teaching, and he is honored as the first person in China to encourage education for everyone, rather than just the children of nobles.

In the end, teaching is why this ancient master's wisdom survived. Conversations between Confucius and his students, along with many wise sayings, were recorded in the Analects of Confucius. Five other books—containing history, rituals, poetry, and governing policies—are also traditionally attributed to Confucius. Modern scholars, however, suspect that others wrote or compiled several of these texts.

Throughout the Warring States period, many people yearned for the social and political stability Confucius promised. So his lessons passed from one generation to the next, all the while being refined and expanded. When the Han Dynasty took hold, rulers recognized the power of these teachings—particularly regarding the Mandate

of Heaven—in supporting their authority. The classics of Confucius then became the foundation for any education. Temples sprang up, and historians wrote the earliest biographies of the long-deceased philosopher. Confucius had finally made it.

Millennia later Confucian ideas are known worldwide. Confucian values—particularly the emphasis on mutual respect, cooperation for the benefit of society, and obedience to parents and authority figures—remain important to Chinese identity.

TAOISM YIELDS HARMONY

Scholars disagree about whether Lao-tzu, the founder of Taoism, really existed. If he did, the story goes that he was a librarian in the Zhou court who tired of watching the tumult of a dynasty in decline. Lao-tzu quit his post and decided to leave the empire altogether. As he neared China's border, a guard at the mountain pass begged him to write down his teachings, which resulted in the Tao Te Ching, the primary text of Taoism. Having left this gift behind, Lao-tzu was never heard from again.

Biographers recorded the story of Lao-tzu's life long after his death; so modern-day scholars suspect that someone else recorded the pithy proverbs in the Tao Te Ching. In fact, many ideas in this book date back to before Lao-tzu was supposedly born, during the time of the

Lao-tzu honored the *Tao*, or the Way, which cannot be fully defined and yet is the energy behind all things.

Hundred Schools of Thought. Based on his story, Lao-tzu was loath to seek fame for himself. Yet someone recognized that attributing the Tao Te Ching to a writer whose name, Lao-tzu, meant "Old Master" would increase the value of the lessons inside.

One biographer records Confucius seeking out Lao-tzu at the Zhou court, with the younger scholar being awed by the presence of the elder. "At last I may say that I have seen a dragon," Confucius reportedly said. "My mouth fell open and I couldn't close it; my tongue flew up and I couldn't even stammer." Lao-tzu's reaction was just the opposite. When Confucius complained that seventy-two kings had been unmoved by his ideas, Lao-tzu advised him to give up ambitious pride and quit trying to enforce overbearing rules.

Taoism encourages people to embrace the natural life force of the universe, called the Tao. Doing so means accepting how the world is and living in harmony with both its predictable patterns and constant change. Some people misinterpret Taoist teachings to mean that the best course of action is inaction, letting life take care of itself. Rather, the idea is to weigh each decision for how it reflects the Tao. Then any action taken or not taken feels genuine and effortless. "Perfect activity leaves no track behind it," the Tao Te Ching says. "Perfect speech is like a jade worker whose tool leaves no mark."

An important part of Taoism is recognizing that opposing forces are essential to each other. "When the world knows beauty as beauty, ugliness arises," the Tao Te Ching says. "Difficult and easy bring about each other. Long and short reveal each other. High and low support each other." The yin and yang symbol, in which black and white shapes flow together to form a perfectly balanced circle, represents this principle.

Confucianism as a philosophy outlines values for living in society. Taoism began as a philosophy and then transformed into a religion through which people also explore—often through ritual—their place in the universe and relationship with

nature. Becoming one with the Tao, or the Way, is the path to eternal life, and reaching this goal is not easy. It is possible, however, as illustrated by the Eight Immortals, who began their lives as mortal humans. The earliest known portraits of these Taoist deities are found in tombs dated to the Jin Dynasty of the twelfth to thirteenth centuries. Each figure is associated with a different arena of life and has specific attributes for identification. For example, Hé Xiāngū, the only woman in the group, carries a branch with fruit or a flowering plant and is the patron of housewives. With his flute, Hán Xiāngzi supports musicians.

In popular Taoism, the Eight Immortals include young and old, rich and poor to convey the idea that immortality is accessible to anyone.

Early Taoists worshipped emperors and Lao-tzu as gods, alongside ancient local deities. Throughout history, China's diverse population has had countless folk religions, which are faiths practiced by small groups of people. If all the modern followers of Chinese folk religions were combined into one group, however, then they would represent one of the largest religions in the world. Each of these groups has its own set of deities. The Naxi people of southwestern China, for example, believe that every part of nature contains a living spirit. Nature- and weather-inspired deities are common in folk religions, as are gods and goddesses representing cities, heroes, and dragons. Taoism embraces these folk deities.

Despite their differences, Confucianism and Taoism have much in common. Both belief systems argue that the best way for individuals to improve society is to first improve themselves. Both teach that every part of the universe is interconnected and arranged in a natural order. During dynastic times, both reinforced the idea that em-

This earthen mound covers the burial chamber of Qin Shi Huangdi. Archaeologists hope to use modern technologies to explore the tomb without disturbing it.

perors were divinely ordained. Taoism even portrayed heaven like a well-organized bureaucracy. It advised rulers to rid themselves of unnatural ambition and to give subjects as much freedom as possible. "So long as I act only by inactivity," a Taoist saying goes, "the people will of themselves become prosperous."

In general, Taoism was well supported through the dynasties. Rulers of the Tang Dynasty even claimed to be descended from Lao-tzu because they shared the same family name of Li. Among other values, Taoism's Three Treasures—the virtues of compassion, moderation, and humility—are at the heart of Chinese culture.

HONORING ANCESTORS BRINGS GOOD FORTUNE

Chinese peoples have demonstrated their belief in the afterlife from the first Neolithic burials that contained grave goods. The most famous tomb is that of Shi Huangdi of the Qin Dynasty. In 1974 farmers digging a well came face-to-face with

In 1974, a farmer discovered the first terracotta warrior, part of an army of life-size figures serving Qin Shi Huangdi in the afterlife.

an almost life-sized warrior made of terracotta, which is a type of pottery. The emperor had himself buried with an army of more than eight thousand soldier statues, plus clay bureaucratic officials, servants, horses, and acrobats. A first-century historian from the Han Dynasty claimed the emperor's coffin was surrounded by a model of the empire and universe—with replicas of court buildings, rivers of liquid mercury flowing through the landscape, and the heavens charted on the ceiling. Although archaeologists have excavated parts of the burial complex, the emperor's tomb chamber remains untouched under an earthen mound that is two hundred fifty feet tall.

The symbolism of these preparations goes beyond showing off a person's wealth. According to Chinese folk religions, ancestors remain connected to the world's affairs even in death. Paying respect to ancestors honors how they brought the living—and the world they inhabit—into existence. It also ensures that ancestors are well cared for in the afterlife, where they continue to look out for the living. With this view, tremendous tribute was due to Qin Shi Huangdi, who unified the war-ridden territories of ancient China. The tomb also illustrates how Qin Shi Huangdi did not plan to retire upon his death. He needed everything around him to continue overseeing an empire in the afterlife.

Satisfied ancestors offer wisdom and send blessings to descendants. In times of need, they also put in a good word with the gods, to whom mortals cannot appeal directly. Ancestors who are not well cared for become known as hungry ghosts, who may become vengeful as they wander about seeking food and other offerings.

Devout families honor ancestors both at temples and in their homes. A home shrine may include ancestors' portraits or written names. Small offerings of food, incense, and fresh flowers are put out year-round. People may bow or kneel before the altars to show respect. Particularly during holidays people burn colorful slips of

paper, called joss paper, that look like pretend money. Burning the slips of paper transfers this ghost money to the spirit realm where ancestors can use it.

Ancestor worship is an important part of China's most famous festivals. Chinese New Year is celebrated in January or February in connection with the lunar calendar. During this time, what is usually a small shelf of offerings becomes an entire table laden with food, including the ancestors' favorite dishes and foods with symbolic meaning. The New Year dinner when family gathers together is the biggest feast of the year, and the celebration continues for weeks afterward. Traditionally communities worked together to sponsor fireworks, dragon and lion dances, theatrical performances, and other cultural activities.

Lion dances, fireworks, special foods, and family gatherings are all part of Lunar New Year celebrations.

From the fourth through tenth centuries, thousands of caves across northern China became Buddhist shrines. Later, people removed many heads like these from shrine statues to sell to art collectors.

BUDDHISM OFFERS SALVATION

Buddhism began around the same time as Confucianism and Taoism, but in a region that is now Nepal and India. Tradition tells the story of a prince who never encountered suffering until he explored the world beyond his palace walls. When the prince witnessed the sorrow of an old man, a sick man, and a dead man, he no longer wanted his life of luxury. He cut his long hair, removed his bejeweled earrings, and traded his lavish garments for simple robes. The prince wandered for years, reflecting on the experience of life. One day, while meditating under a tree, he found enlightenment—a truth that allowed him to discard human desires. Ever since, this prince has been known as the Buddha. During his lifetime, the Buddha's wisdom attracted loyal followers and disciples who spread his teachings.

Merchants and monks traveling from India and Central Asia along the Silk Road brought Buddhism to China around the first century AD. Five centuries later, Buddhism was as popular as the homegrown Taoism. People liked the promise of salvation, which Buddhism made available to anyone, while original Taoist teachings reserved immortality for a select few. It is not a coincidence that Taoism's Eight Immortals, who made salvation more accessible to all, first appeared as Buddhism gained followers. This is just one example of how the two religions borrowed from and influenced each other in China.

Buddhism teaches that every action someone takes evokes *karma*, which is a cosmic force that brings reward or punishment. When a person dies, the karma built up by good or bad acts in their current lifetime determines how their soul will be reborn in the next life. Individuals with good karma may be reborn in heavenly realms. Those with bad karma may be reborn as animals or in hell-like realms. The ultimate goal is to reach *nirvana*, a state of enlightenment that allows a soul to finally escape this cycle of death and rebirth.

To reach enlightenment, Buddha's followers must understand the Four Noble Truths. The first is that suffering always exists. Even when people are free from illness or loss, they continue to suffer because humans are imperfect. The second truth is that this ongoing suffering comes from human desire. The imperfect world is bound to disappoint when it does not live up to a person's expectations. The third truth is that people can release themselves from suffering by freeing themselves from desire. The fourth truth is that the path to becoming free of desire involves gaining wisdom, acting ethically, and cultivating mental discipline.

After Buddha died about twenty-five hundred years ago, a council of monks tried to create a doctrine for all Buddhists to follow. When they couldn't agree, Buddhism split into many schools, each adding its own teachings, texts, and ways of worship. As a result, Buddhism has many forms of prayer, including *mantras*, which are

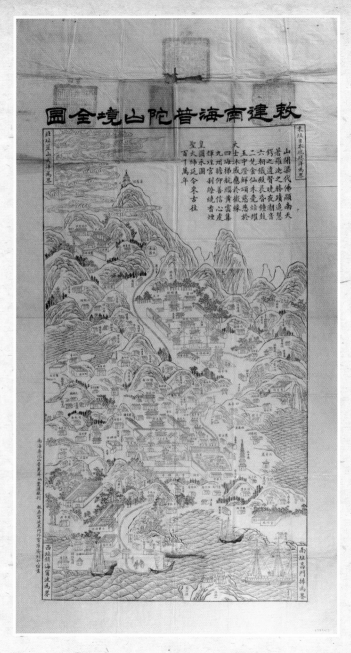

This nineteenth-century map leads pilgrims to shrines on Mount Putuo,
one of four mountains in China that Buddhists hold sacred.

powerful phrases that may be chanted silently or aloud. Followers seek guidance from the Buddha and numerous *bodhisattvas,* who are beings that have achieved enlightenment but remain on Earth to help mortals.

Some Buddhist texts promise rewards for making or sponsoring images of Buddha. The more people invest, the faster their souls advance toward nirvana. Emperors who dedicated palaces full of precious things to Buddha may even have reached enlightenment with this single act. Common people made progress with smaller devotions. This explains why in sixth-century China, royal and wealthy families paid for large-scale temples and statues, while peasants donated nearly half of the statues in Buddhist monasteries.

Pilgrimages are another way to show devotion. This tradition began in South Asia with believers who hoped to gain blessings or have divinely inspired visions by journeying to the sites that were important to the Buddha's life. As Buddhism spread, pilgrimage sites cropped up in other countries. Mount Putuo, on a coastal island in Zhejiang Province, illustrates how the Chinese blended faiths together over time. This mountain was already sacred for Taoists when Buddhism arrived in China, and other Chinese traditions say mountains are where heaven and Earth touch. Buddhists believe bodhisattvas live on sacred mountains. Beginning about AD 1000, visitors to Mount Putuo talked of seeing the bodhisattva of mercy and compassion, named Guanyin. Word got around and by the 1800s, millions of pilgrims visited Mount Putuo annually.

Guanyin is a powerful Buddhist deity. An ancient scripture described a bodhisattva who could change into thirty-three different forms to answer devotees' prayers as quickly as possible. This deity changes identity and gender depending on region, time period, and context. In Tibet, the Dalai Lama is believed to be the incarnation of this deity. In most of China, however, this bodhisattva is known as Guanyin. The Water-Moon Guanyin reminds worshippers that the world is as elusive as moonlight

Buddhism has many bodhisattvas, each with their own focus and personality. The Thousand-Armed Guanyin (*right*) helps people with almost any struggle.

on water. The Child-Giving Guanyin aids women who want to have children. The Thousand-Armed Guanyin helps people with almost any struggle.

Buddhism took hold in China as the Han Dynasty crumbled. As often happens, new rulers reject the philosophies of the old, and Confucianism temporarily fell from favor as people turned more to Taoism and Buddhism. For centuries the pendulum of acceptance swung back and forth. Buddhism was especially vulnerable to politics when temples or monasteries appeared to have more financial assets or influence than rulers. Monasteries tried to protect themselves from harassment by local officials by cultivating powerful patrons. A stone carving in front of a temple bearing the name of an important magistrate could serve the temple's needs, while also helping the named official gain merit toward nirvana.

Sometimes safeguards were not enough. The Three Disasters of Wu refer to occasions between AD 400 and AD 900 when Buddhism was banned by emperors

The Longmen Grottoes have more than twenty-three-hundred limestone niches carved into shrines, with Buddhist statues ranging from one inch to fifty-seven feet tall.

in different dynasties, who coincidentally each had *Wu* as part of their names. Each time the emperor believed monasteries to be more motivated by collecting money or wielding political sway than in promoting prayer. Monasteries were closed, assets confiscated, and monks and nuns forced to return to civilian life. Sometimes these persecutions involved violence.

From the fourth through tenth centuries AD, thousands of rock faces and caves across northern China were turned into Buddhist shrines. These remote and hidden locations made it easier to worship away from imperial eyes. Some sites held one hundred thousand carvings and paintings, ranging from an inch to over fifty feet tall.

After each of these periods, Buddhism made a comeback—usually after an emperor ascended who was either a Buddhist himself or who felt secure enough to support religious tolerance. Thus Buddhism remained an ongoing influence, and for centuries Chinese peoples continued to blend its practices and beliefs with those of other systems.

IMAGINE BEING A PILGRIM AT MOUNT TAI . . .

You are traveling with a group of women that was organized by a matchmaker. None of you has traveled away from home before, and this journey may be the only opportunity in your lifetime to see the world beyond your village.

When you arrive, you find yourself among thousands of women also seeking the blessings of health and fertility for the future. Mount Tai, one of the five sacred mountains of Taoism, is home to Bixia Yuanjun, the Goddess of the Dawn who watches over each child's birth. The mountain also has temples for the Goddess of Fertility and the Goddess of Eyesight. The more embroidered eye masks your group places at the temple for the Goddess of Eyesight, the stronger her healing powers will be.

IMAGINE BEING A NUN OR MONK . . .

Since taking orders, you have shaved your head as a sign of your commitment to holy life. In addition to studying religious texts and praying, you spend your days maintaining temples, helping others make their offerings, and aiding those in need.

As a nun, you most likely joined the nunnery as a teen because your family did not have funds for a dowry, or you joined as a widow, after your children were grown. Either way, this life has brought you education and independence that you would not have had otherwise. As a monk, you may have taken orders at any age at which you were inspired, even if it meant leaving a wife and children at home.

A Jesuit missionary's tombstone included Latin and Chinese inscriptions.

CHRISTIANITY

According to an ancient carved stone, a Christian missionary first reached China in AD 635 and founded a church with the emperor's approval. About two hundred years later, Emperor Wuzong of the Tang Dynasty banned Christianity, along with all foreign faiths, and confiscated church resources. This cycle of acceptance and rejection went on for centuries.

As the age of exploration brought Europeans into more frequent contact with other parts of the world, an order of Catholic priests, called Jesuits, was founded in 1534 with a strong emphasis on missionary work. Jesuits were educated in mathematics, sciences, and arts. They realized that the key to success in China was cultivating support among scholar-officials and accommodating local customs, such as translating Catholic prayer books into local languages. Through their work, Christianity slowly gained a foothold in China.

This Catholic prayer book is written in Yi, a local script from southwest China.

A cap worn by Sufi Muslims during the Qing Dynasty

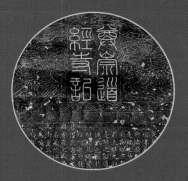

A stele from one of China's earliest synagogues, founded in AD 1163

ISLAM

Muslims in China today trace their heritage back to the Tang and Song Dynasties, when trade regularly brought merchants to China from Central Asia and the Middle East. Under the Mongolian rulers of the Yuan Dynasty, the empire stretched far enough into these lands that it included places where Islam was common, and Muslim subjects also moved throughout the empire as government administrators. Being Muslim in China today can mean many things. Some are Muslim by ancestry but do not practice Islam.

JUDAISM

Judaism also came to China along with merchants on the Silk Road. By the twelfth century AD, a synagogue was built in Kaifeng, which was a major trading hub and the empire's capital for a time. In the twentieth century, Shanghai became a place of refuge during the Holocaust, receiving an estimated forty thousand people. Many of those immigrants moved again after World War II to escape the turmoil of China's civil war during that time.

The jade belt at this puppet's waist likely signals that he is a god, an official, or a noble.

SHARING STORIES ACROSS TIME: SHADOW PUPPETRY

The rich history of China's philosophies and faiths has spawned countless stories of suffering and success. For thousands of years these tales were passed along to a mostly illiterate population through traditions of oral storytelling, rituals, and visual and performing arts. Shadow puppetry was a perfect fit for such morality plays. "Shadows are associated with people's souls, whether the person is living or dead," explains Dr. Mia Yinxing Liu, an art historian at Bates College in Maine. "So a play made of shadows becomes the perfect threshold to connect the living and the dead."

The origins of shadow puppetry in China are a mystery. One legend claims it began in the Han Dynasty, when an emperor was distraught over the death of a beloved concubine and offered a reward to anyone who could raise her from the dead. A magician responded by cutting out an image of the woman and making the silhouette dance for the emperor behind a lit screen.

Yet the earliest historical accounts of shadow plays don't occur until centuries later in the Song Dynasty. By this time, shadow plays were performed throughout the countryside, closely linked to the rhythms of farming life. Between cycles of planting and harvesting, peasants enjoyed this affordable entertainment, which required few performers and little setup. Puppets performed fantastical tales of adventure, romance, and the supernatural. They followed epic journeys of human heroes, immortals, and gods. During busy months, special performances were organized to pray for rain or protection from locusts.

Shadow theater was originally performed in the open air, at night, with the stage open to the village temple altar so gods could enjoy the show, too. Later, in the Ming dynasty, it became popular for wealthy families to hire private performances to mark important events. Themes might be to thank the gods for recovery

from illness or to bless the construction of a new house. "Shadow theater served as a ritual of prayer and thanksgiving," Dr. Liu says, "because it provided a channel between humanity and gods."

Early shadow puppets were made of paper or plant leaves. Later people soaked animal skins that they then stretched and scraped to become transparent parchment. After being cut, the puppet's body parts were buffed and polished again. Then they were painted with intricate designs, varnished, and assembled. Working behind white screens, performers used wire and sticks to animate the puppets. Oil lamps were placed strategically so that puppets cast the only shadows.

The see-through quality of the puppets, along with the flickering of lamplight, made this art form mystical. "Imagine watching these performances at night, on a screen that was illuminated to set itself apart from the darkness," Dr. Liu says. "The light made the puppets, which are inanimate objects, come alive. Audiences were enchanted."

Top: Light shines through these puppets made of animal hides to project bright colors onto a screen. *Bottom*: Chinese Theatre Works, a contemporary shadow-puppet troupe from New York, performs an act from *Journey to the West*.

公孫霸 黒長満髯

第四章

CHAPTER FOUR

This seventh century AD mural depicts court officials greeting visitors from foreign lands, who bring gifts for the emperor. Paying tribute was important in establishing trade with China.

世界的中国

ON THE WORLD STAGE

A POWERHOUSE OF TRADE AND EXCHANGE

All through the age of exploration, which began in the 1400s, western Europeans viewed China as isolated by mountains, deserts, and sheer distance from themselves. Although China's goods were highly desirable, the country had a reputation for being closed off to new ideas and reluctant to interact with other societies.

A broader view of history, however, reveals that China was built by constant innovation and the adoption and blending of diverse cultural traditions. China's earliest dynastic rulers focused on establishing authority, trade patterns, and defenses close to home. The fact that Inner Mongolia, Sichuan, Manchuria, and dozens of other regions were once separate states—each comprised of dozens of distinct

societies—is easily forgotten when for centuries maps have showed them as part of a unified China. For perspective, consider that all the distinct languages, governments, and cultures of Europe—from the United Kingdom and into Russia as far as the Ural Mountains—could almost fit within the borders of modern China.

When what was called the Far East first met what could equally be described as the Far West through the Silk Road in the first century BC, the Han Empire was twice the size of the Roman Empire. China also was more commercially advanced in having the manufacturing capacity to serve large markets. For centuries, trade over land and sea flourished and China was the wealthiest nation in the world.

When two centers of power collide, it is not surprising that conflict occurs. China's rulers eventually turned inward—shunning foreign exchange just as Europe entered the era of colonization and the Industrial Revolution. Suddenly China fell behind, and the pace of change was moving faster than ever before. The last emperor fell in 1911, bringing an end to dynastic rule in China. Over the course of the twentieth century, China has reorganized its government. In recent decades it has reasserted its historical role as a trading partner on the world stage.

TRAVELING THE SILK ROAD

When Chinese silk first reached the Mediterranean world, ancient Romans had no idea where it came from. They only knew this rare luxury could be acquired through trade routes that went far, far to the east. Meanwhile China didn't know the dramatic distances its silk traveled until Han Dynasty rulers sent a diplomatic mission far, far to the west. Once the connection was made, new opportunities for economic and cultural exchange blossomed.

Trade routes along the Silk Road offered as much peril as they did profit. For thousands of miles, paths edged China's Taklamakan Desert and crossed some of the highest mountain ranges on Earth. Weather, war, and bandits forced changes to

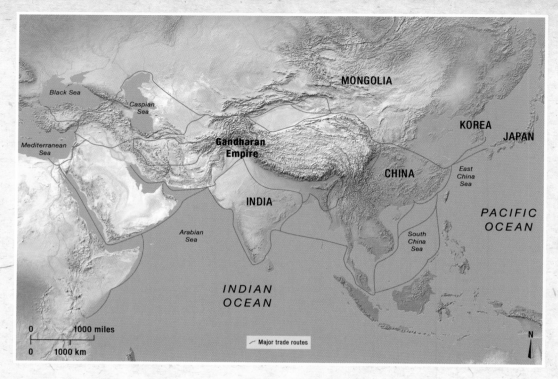

The Silk Road was a vast network of shifting routes used by soldiers, pilgrims, migrants, and merchants to travel between ancient China and the eastern Mediterranean.

trade routes from year to year. In times of peace, imperial soldiers patrolled remote roads. In times of turmoil, emperors recalled the troops—leaving travelers, traders, and pilgrims to fend for themselves.

During the height of Silk Road trade, from the third to tenth centuries AD, merchants carried travel passes listing the people, animals, and goods that accompanied them. From these firsthand accounts, modern historians know that few people traveled the full expanse from China to the Mediterranean. Instead most merchants traveled in small groups through specific territories and then exchanged goods with others who covered the next stretch. Donkeys were dependable in mountainous

terrain, horses were efficient in smooth grasslands, and two-humped Bactrian camels were ideal for trekking through harsh deserts.

Nestled among the mountainous sand dunes, oasis towns offered survival and refuge. These settlements arose where underground rivers bubbled to the surface or were at least close enough to reach with wells. Besides weary travelers, the precious liquid of life supported garrisons of soldiers, irrigation farming, and permanent communities. Scholars estimate twenty-eight languages were spoken in settlements surrounding the Taklamakan Desert, making these oases lively centers of cultural—as well as commercial—exchange.

One such oasis town was Dunhuang, which was nearly forgotten when the Silk Road declined. Dunhuang is now famous for the thousands of elaborate paintings adorning hundreds of caves that Buddhist monks had dug into nearby cliffs. In 1900 a secret library was discovered from behind a crumbling cave wall. Forty thousand neatly tied silk and paper scrolls contained important texts from Buddhism and other religions. After being hidden for centuries, these manuscripts revealed the cosmopolitan atmosphere of this frontier town.

Archaeologists renewed interest in Dunhuang, an almost forgotten Silk Road oasis, after the 1900 discovery of an ancient library with more than forty thousand scrolls.

Imports to China from the Silk Road included precious gems, spices, and unique materials to make perfumes and cosmetics. Emperors also sought horses for their cavalries, since these animals were native to the bordering mountains and steppes

but not central China. The most common items offered in exchange were bolts of silk, which were easy to carry and highly valued because for centuries only China knew how to extract the threads from silkworms' precious cocoons. In the eighth century AD, market inspectors at the oasis town of Turfan recorded that twenty bolts of silk bought a strong horse.

The Silk Road also channeled an exchange of ideas and technologies. Eventually paper made its way to Europe, along with the secret of silk. Buddhism came to China, along with cotton farming and the Western custom of sitting on chairs. The abacus, a tool for calculating great numbers with just a few beads, tallied accounts on both ends of the continent.

The abacus tallied accounts in China and the Middle East. Scholars don't know if this tool developed independently in both regions or if it was spread through cultural exchange.

The Tang Dynasty, from AD 618 to AD 907, benefitted from the prosperity of the Silk Road and was a time when people were enamored with foreign ways. Great patrons of poetry, music, and art, the Tang ruling house welcomed foreign musicians and performers to their courts. Fashions from what were considered barbarian peoples outside imperial borders were popular, and about one-third of the residents in the Tang capital of Chang'an were foreign.

Increased trade also led to increased conflict. To control trade routes, the Tang pushed the imperial borders north of Tibet and as far west as modern-day Uzbekistan. In AD 751, however, Arab military forces decisively defeated the Tang army at the Battle of Talas, ending that dynasty's ambitions in Central Asia. Shortly thereafter Tang troops were called home to quash the An Lushan Rebellion, which was one of the largest in China's history. They were also needed to block foreign intrusions into the empire's core territory.

During the Song Dynasty from AD 960 to AD 1279, restrictions on buying and selling relaxed, and traders no longer had to operate in imperially approved markets. This, combined with booming production, encouraged markets to spread throughout the country. So much business was being transacted that the Song Dynasty printed the world's first paper money to facilitate trade.

Agriculture at this time benefitted from a major population shift plus new varieties of crops. Ever since Neolithic times, most of China's population had lived in northern territories. During the Tang Dynasty, 60 percent of people did so. Then frequent attacks from northern nomadic tribes forced a mass relocation, and by the Song Dynasty, 60 percent of the population lived in the south. This was rice-growing country, and farmers had just developed a new rice that grew quickly enough to harvest two crops a year. Food production swelled, giving farmers more flexibility to grow cash crops such as lychees and tangerines. Farmers also began producing handicrafts and participating in markets.

The Song Dynasty was a blossoming of Chinese society from economic, artistic, manufacturing, agricultural, and intellectual perspectives. Even without the northern territories—which nomadic tribes ruled through the Jin and Liao Dynasties—the Song Empire was likely the wealthiest country in the world during its time.

Mongols reunified the land and founded the Yuan dynasty around AD 1279. Foreigners who were famous for their fast horses and accurate archers, the Mongols

The Battle of Yehuling, in AD 1211, was one of the Mongols' first victories over the Jin Dynasty. By AD 1271, Mongols had conquered nearly all of China.

managed an empire that encompassed Silk Road routes from China to the Mediterranean Sea. Their capital city entertained visitors from Russia, Syria, France, Germany, Hungary, and many other nations. The famous Marco Polo visited Emperor Kublai Khan at the Yuan court. Although some scholars question whether this Italian explorer made it all the way to China, others say that his journals about Chinese paper currency and methods for making salt are too detailed to have been written from hearsay.

The Mongols favored their own customs over those of the Chinese. Being better warriors than they were administrators, however, they soon recognized the benefits of China's imperial bureaucracy and adopted those strategies for governing. Unfortunately they let Chinese arts and other traditions wither. The end of the Yuan Dynasty in 1368 marked the decline of safe travel along the Silk Road—and left a lingering distrust of foreign rule.

CERAMICS ON THE HIGH SEAS

Although lightweight silk traveled well by land, heavy ceramics and cast-iron bars were more easily transported by sea to destinations in Southeast Asia, India, the Middle East, and East Africa. By the Tang Dynasty, maritime trade in China was busy enough for emperors to appoint a superintendent of shipping trade to collect duties and coordinate translations at seaports.

Maritime voyages were less susceptible to politics because dominating the open seas was harder than controlling narrow mountain passages. Nonetheless these trade routes had their own unique hazards. "Shipwrecks are an important source of

This photo from the *Java Sea Shipwreck* underwater excavation shows how the archaeologists lay out a grid and number every object, even when excavating underwater.

information," says Dr. Lisa Niziolek, an archaeologist at The Field Museum. "A single wreck offers a snapshot of what commodities were being traded and helps us investigate how goods were manufactured. Analyzed together, many shipwrecks reveal major shifts in social and economic relationships."

Artifacts that do not decay in water can last for centuries hidden beneath the waves. Once found, however, they can be hard to retrieve because water can be deep, excavations are expensive, and sites are hard to protect from looters. One shipwreck found in the waters between Java and Sumatra illustrates this well. This sunken vessel was first spied in the 1980s by fishermen who noticed birds diving for dinner far from land. The birds were attracted to fish hiding among the eight-hundred-year-old wreckage. Once spotted, the shipwreck attracted human looters for years before a salvage company secured approval from the Indonesian government to begin archaeological investigations. Since the ship's wooden hull and masts had long since rotted, divers spent two months retrieving more durable objects from the ocean floor and mapping the site. Before analysis the mostly ceramic and iron artifacts required months of soaking in freshwater baths to draw out ocean salts that could cause deterioration when exposed to air.

About half of the twelve thousand artifacts recovered went to the Indonesian government and half were donated to Chicago's Field Museum. Dr. Niziolek has studied the fourteen hundred covered boxes and thousands of other ceramics found at the site. "At first, they all looked very similar," she says. "But when you look closely, there is huge variety." The boxes represent different shapes and sizes, have different glazes, and are decorated with flowers, fish, dragons, and geometric designs. Researchers estimate that the wrecked ship may have carried up to one hundred thousand ceramic pieces, demonstrating both the international demand for Chinese ceramics and the scale of Chinese manufacturing.

Other parts of the world had ceramics at that time, but none could produce as high a quality for so low a cost. Until the eighteenth century, only China had the resources and expertise to produce porcelain. "Everyone wanted porcelain because it was so functional and beautiful," Dr. Niziolek says. "This shipwreck shows that China was producing porcelain on a massive enough scale to supply markets in Africa, Asia, and Europe."

Chemical analysis of the ceramics shows that some pieces from this ship came from Jingdezhen, in Jiangxi Province, which was the capital of porcelain production centuries ago and remains so today. The ceramics were fired in kilns that could hold about twenty thousand pieces at a time. A workshop could employ hundreds, even thousands, of craftsmen, and entire villages were dedicated to this industry. Some

At The Field Museum, each artifact is analyzed to learn about the ceramic industry and trade patterns of thirteenth-century China. Liz Haake helped to photograph and catalog more than 7,500 pieces from the *Java Sea Shipwreck*.

families put their names or production locations on pieces made in their workshops. "Just as we see 'Made in China' on the bottom of coffee mugs today," Dr. Niziolek says, "almost eight hundred years ago manufacturers marked their products in a similar fashion. This is their advertising." In addition to the highest quality of porcelain, the ship carried ceramics that were less expensive but were designed to mimic the color and finish of the best—indicating that merchants had a sophisticated understanding of the marketplace and offered products at every price level.

The *Java Sea Shipwreck* vessel also held almost two hundred tons of iron bars—the most ever found on a trading vessel from this period. In the ninth through eleventh centuries, China's annual output of iron increased six-fold, reaching a rate of production that Europe did not achieve until the eighteenth century. Some scientists wonder if the weight of its cargo caused this ship to founder in a storm.

Researchers aren't sure where this ship was headed, but one likely place is Tuban, an ancient trading port on the island of Java. The vessel's contents support evidence that China was enmeshed in a complex network that connected many societies. The iron was probably bound for Indonesia. Chinese ceramic boxes from the Song and Yuan Dynasties have turned up in twenty countries. And the ship itself, based on analysis of tiny bits of wood that survived, was likely built in Southeast Asia. For Dr. Niziolek, the hours, weeks, and months spent studying ceramics are about connecting to these people from the past. She asks questions about who made items, who transported them, and who purchased them. "My research is really about understanding how complicated these human relationships can be," she says.

When the Ming Dynasty began in 1368, sea commerce took on a different role. The Ming represented a return to Han Chinese rule, after a century of being ruled by the foreign Yuan. As part of the effort to resurrect Chinese values and traditions, early Ming emperors adopted the historically dim view of traders. Periodically, private trading with foreigners was banned (although rules were often broken), and ap-

proved trading was restricted to certain ports. As the yoke of foreign authority grew more distant, the Ming once again permitted foreign trade but under a watchful eye.

The Ming Dynasty is famous for diplomatic seafaring voyages that were designed to impress and inspire tribute from potential trading partners. From 1405 to 1433, the Ming sent fleets of one hundred ships and nearly twenty-seven thousand men abroad in seven voyages that visited Java, Sri Lanka, India, the Middle East, and Kenya. The vessels themselves were probably about two hundred feet long. By comparison, the three ships Christopher Columbus later took on his transatlantic voyage were each about eighty feet long.

Admiral Zheng He, who was a Muslim and a eunuch, led the Ming expeditions. Zheng He came to the Ming court as a boy when he was captured during the over-

No design plans survived to the present day, so this model of a Ming treasure vessel is based on shipwrecks from the era.

throw of the Yuan Dynasty. As the emperor's representative, Zheng He negotiated the exchange of goods, oversaw improvements to foreign trading ports, and communicated the emperor's disdain for those who did not welcome the fleet. He also encouraged foreign leaders to send tribute to the emperor, including giraffes, lions, rhinoceroses, ostriches, and leopards.

These voyages stopped after the death of the emperor who commissioned them. Later Ming emperors declared them to have been an extravagance that emptied imperial coffers. In hindsight, pulling back on seafaring just as it became a force of world domination was a mistake. The expectation that other countries would come to China for commerce backfired when those nations wanted to establish their own trading bases on Chinese soil.

Ming emperors initially rejected the Portuguese, who landed in China in 1517 after having just captured Malacca, a port in the nearby kingdom of Malay. After decades of tussling, the Ming eventually let Portugal manage the southern port city of Macau, which it promptly built a wall around. Sometimes trade continued at a brisk pace and sometimes Ming emperors imposed limits as they grew increasingly wary about the motives of foreign traders.

"People often interpret China's reluctance for international interaction

A Ming emperor commissioned Admiral Zheng He's voyages, but forty years after his last voyage, Ming Dynasty officials destroyed all records of them. People debate whether Zheng He (above) brought honor to the empire or drained its treasury.

at this time as coming from pride," Dr. Niziolek says. Another possibility is that emperors distanced themselves from nations that they suspected wanted to do more than trade. In response emperors promoted classic teachings that celebrated domestic production and self-reliance. "Sometimes when two sides are in conflict," Dr. Niziolek says, "the fighting groups look more inward because they are trying to live up to their own ideals."

POWER IN SLOW DECLINE

During the Ming Dynasty, China sold more goods than it bought, bringing in a steady influx of silver coins, minted in Mexico, to supplement its own currency. Then, when politics abroad interfered with this trade, the Ming did not have the ships or the colonies to protect China's interests. They struggled to pay for military campaigns in the north that seemed unending. They also strained to collect taxes during an unprecedented streak of natural disasters. In 1556, for example, Shaanxi Province experienced the deadliest earthquake in recorded history: cracks sixty feet deep fractured the earth's surface, entire cities crumbled, and an estimated eight hundred thirty thousand people died. Then in 1642 local officials destroyed a levy in order to quash a rebellion. Raging waters from the Yellow River, and the famine and plague that followed, killed around three hundred thousand people.

Despite these woes, the Ming poured wealth into their lavish courts. One emperor supported more than seventy thousand eunuchs and ten thousand women in his palace. Others built and renovated the nearly one thousand palace and court buildings of Beijing's Forbidden City—so named because ordinary people were not allowed in this sacred space of the emperor. Eventually these extravagances distracted emperors from their duties and allowed overambitious advisers too much authority.

Beijing's imperial court, called the Forbidden City, was the center of power for nearly five hundred years during the Ming and Qing dynasties.

Meanwhile, just north of the empire, another group was gaining power. In 1644 after conquering the Mongol tribes and recruiting defectors from Ming armies, the Manchu people conquered the Ming rulers and founded the Qing Dynasty—the last imperial court to rule China. The Qing were more adaptable to Chinese customs than some of the previous foreign rulers and incorporated officials from the former Ming court into their administration from the beginning. During their reign, the Qing added the territories of Mongolia, Manchuria, Tibet, and Xinjiang to the empire. They also experimented with New World crops, using maize, sweet potatoes, peanuts, and potatoes to cultivate land that had not supported traditional Chinese crops. This led to another burst for agriculture, the economy, and the population.

Underneath this success, however, China began to lose its edge in technology. Beginning in the 1700s, the Industrial Revolution—a shift to harnessing the power of

machines to perform work humans had previously done by hand—spread through Europe and the Americas. Experts debate why China's early technological expertise and experience with mass production did not lead to an Industrial Revolution on its own soil first. Did Chinese academies spend too much time on Confucian ideals that emphasized tradition and not enough time teaching the scientific method of inquiry? Perhaps China's huge population gave it less incentive than other countries to do more with fewer people. Whatever the reason, the result of this shift was that other parts of the world came to produce greater quantities and varieties of goods more efficiently. Thus other countries built great wealth at the same time they were inventing new types of weapons and defense systems. As had constantly happened throughout history, the world was changing. This time, however, China was not at the forefront.

DYNASTIC RULE COMES TO AN END

The Qing were generally suspicious of trade with Europeans. One official once described the English, French, Dutch, Spanish, and Portuguese as "dark, dangerous, and inscrutable; wherever they go they spy around with a view to seizing other peoples' lands." Beginning in 1757, the Qing limited all foreign trade to approved merchants going in and out of the southern port city of Guangzhou in Guangdong Province.

Westerners objected, but stability had been restored to China's economy and for a while it still enjoyed the privilege of exporting more than it imported. In the 1790s an envoy from England asked permission to convert a small island off China's coast into a trading base where English merchants could live and store wares. The Qing emperor refused. In a letter to King George III, Emperor Qianlong explained that any trade at all was already providing a favor because "the tea, silk, and porcelain which the Celestial Empire produces are absolute necessities to Europeans." The message

was that Europe needed China, but the feeling wasn't mutual. "Our Celestial Empire possesses all things in prolific abundance and lacks no product within its own borders," the emperor wrote. "There [is] therefore no need to import the manufactures of outside barbarians in exchange for our own produce."

Although disliking the tone of this letter, the British could not deny its contents. Throughout centuries of trade, one of the primary items China had desired from foreign nations was money. Europe, on the other hand, had shown an unquenchable demand for traditional Chinese goods, as well as sugar and tea. Scholars believe tea originated in the region of northeast India and southwest China. It had been unknown in Europe before the seventeenth century. Yet by the time of the British envoy, tea represented half the value of all commodities purchased at Guangzhou. Britain imported about twenty-three million pounds of tea a year, with the taxes on this product providing about one-tenth of the British government's revenues.

Britain wanted better access not just to Chinese products but also to its vast population as a market. Not long after the failed diplomatic mission, Britain discovered a commodity that the Chinese people would buy: opium. Derived from the poppy flower, opium was used as a painkiller at least as early as the eighth century, and

The familiar shape of the teapot emerged during the Ming Dynasty when it became popular to steep tea leaves in boiling water.

Portuguese traders introduced the idea of smoking it in the sixteenth century. Opium, however, is addictive. It interferes with people's ability to think clearly and care for themselves. Seeing people become isolated and eventually die from opium, Qing emperors banned its use and sale. Meanwhile Britain increased poppy farms in colonized India, specifically for selling the illegal drug in China.

Representatives of Queen Victoria and the Qing Emperor Daoguang sign the 1842 Treaty of Nanking, which forced China to open ports for foreign trade.

In the mid-1800s, Qing emperors appointed an imperial official, named Lin Zexu, to crack down on opium smuggling into the southern port of Guangzhou. This minister confiscated twenty thousand chests of opium from British commercial ships and dumped them into the sea. He also published an open letter asking Queen Victoria to curb this disgusting trade. The smugglers, he wrote, "are so obsessed with material

gain that they have no concern whatever for the harm they can cause to others. Have they no conscience? I have heard that you strictly prohibit opium in your own country . . . but you choose to bring that harm to other countries such as China. Why?"

The letter did not spark action, but destroying what was considered the property of British merchants did. A fleet of British gunboats blockaded the Chinese coast until the dispute ended with the 1842 Treaty of Nanking. This agreement forced Qing emperors to open five port cities to foreign trade. It stated that British subjects did not have to follow Chinese law while in China, and it required the Qing Dynasty to pay millions of the silver coins they had imported to compensate traders for lost opium and to reimburse Britain for war costs.

At last Europeans had a solid foothold on Chinese soil and they continued to press their advantage. In 1858 Qing emperors were forced to sign another set of treaties that opened several additional port cities for foreign trade and allowed foreigners to sail boats up the Yangtze River, right into the heart of the country. This treaty actually legalized the opium trade, along with the British practice of transporting Chinese citizens to work in British colonies. Indentured servants from China, as well as India, replaced the cheap labor formerly provided by the Atlantic slave trade, which Britain had ended in 1807. Chinese men were kidnapped or tricked into laboring on sugar plantations, digging in mines, and building railroads. Many did not survive to return home. All in all, treaty demands in connection with the Opium Wars confirmed the worst Chinese suspicions about the motivations of foreigners.

Amidst these intense negotiations, Qing leaders faced one of history's largest and bloodiest civil wars. Previous rebellions had hoped to unseat the Sons of Heaven because they had lost divine favor. The goal of the Taiping Rebellion, beginning in 1850, was to reorganize society by overthrowing Manchu rulers, redistributing land, and promoting equality between men and women. The war raged for fourteen years before the Qing won out, with the help of armies from European trading partners.

A series of rebellions followed, along with a war against Japan in which China lost the island of Taiwan and its strong influence in Korea. During the so-called Boxer Rebellion, from 1899 to 1901, Qing rulers allied themselves with peasants and tried to purge all foreigners from the country. International troops responded by capturing Beijing and requiring reparations. Imperial power never recovered. China's last emperor—a boy of just six years old—was removed from the throne in 1912.

More than three thousand years of dynastic rule in China had ended.

The events that befell the Qing Dynasty did not dramatically differ from what had happened in previous dynasties. The difference this time was that people worldwide had new ideas about the rela-

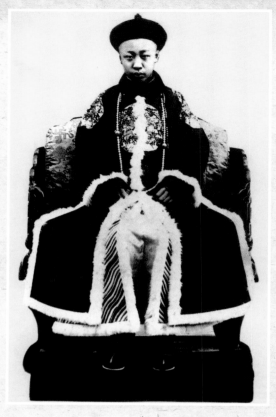

China's last emperor, Puyi, was only six years old when the Qing Dynasty fell in 1912, ending centuries of dynastic rule.

tionships between governments and their people. By the twentieth century, many countries had thrown off the divine rights of kings and created governing systems that included more citizen representation. China was now ready for this, too.

Another entire book could be devoted to the most recent century of Chinese history. From 1912 to 1949 a government called the Republic of China struggled to establish democracy. In 1949 the Communist Party, led by Mao Zedong, created the People's Republic of China. In the aftermath of major social upheaval, along with

Mao Zedong and other Communist officials inaugurated the People's Republic of China at Tiananmen Square on October 1, 1949. This celebrated painting of that scene, created by Chinese artist Dong Xiwen in 1953, is called *The Founding Ceremony of the Nation*.

two world wars, China's new leaders closed the country completely to foreign inter-action for many years. In the following decades, the country made progress toward industrialization but also continued to suffer from widespread famine and restrictive social policies. U.S. President Richard Nixon's visit to China in 1972 is credited with opening a new chapter in the relationship between China and the West. With the death of Mao Zedong in 1976, China's new leaders implemented economic reforms and began to look outward again.

In the final decades of the twentieth century, dramatic industrialization and eco-nomic growth, along with improved international relations, once again established China's position as a world power.

HMS Nemesis—the British navy's first ironclad, steam-powered warship—damages the Chinese fleet during the First Opium War. The ship's name means "archenemy."

IMAGINE BEING IN GUANGZHOU DURING THE OPIUM WARS . . .

You have personally witnessed the tragedy brought by the illegal opium British traders force upon your country. You have watched people throw their lives away—losing interest in family, faith, and livelihood from smoking this drug. As the addiction advances, people's bodies lose the sensation of being hungry, and they waste away in an ugly death.

You were in Guangzhou on the day that Britain sailed its warships against the wind, powered by steam engines, up the Pearl River to attack. You were terrified to realize how inadequate your own navy was against the enemy's state-of-the-art weapons. No matter what the Treaty of Nanking forces you to do, you consider these immoral invaders to be barbarians.

When the Tongzhi Emperor came to the throne at age five, he ruled under the thumb of his mother, Empress Dowager Cixi, who maintained power for almost half a century.

IMAGINE BEING EMPRESS DOWAGER CIXI . . .

You come to court as a teenage concubine and your status rises when you give birth to the emperor's only son. When the emperor dies, his heir is only five years old. Seizing an opportunity, you plot to kill three court advisers who would have controlled your son until he came of age. With the success of this coup, you rule alongside the emperor's widow. Neither of you can sit on the throne yourself. You are called dowager because you have maintained your title of empress after your husband's death. When your son dies from smallpox at age nineteen— with no heir—you adopt a three-year-old nephew to sit on the throne.

Therefore you run state affairs for nearly forty-five years, during a time of great complexity. Your authority withstands popular uprisings, foreign wars, and constant changes in society. Within three years after your death, however, the Qing Dynasty ends.

Paintings were used as makeup guides by performers at the imperial court to create distinct characters. This guide is for a rhinoceros spirit, the 579th character to appear in the play.

CHINESE OPERA

Chinese opera merged longstanding traditions of storytelling, singing, and dancing into an immersive art that makes the tales onstage feel larger-than-life. Before the twentieth century, few people in China could read, so theater helped to share common stories and values. "People gravitated to theater for cultural identity," says Dr. Mia Yinxing Liu of Bates College. "Sometimes it unified people and sometimes it created a venue for defiant activities."

Theater was already well established when an emperor created the first dramatic academy, called Pear Garden, in the eighth century. Ever since, Chinese opera performers have been called Disciples of the Pear Garden. Hundreds of regional styles exist today. Huangmei Opera features light, lyrical songs that were originally about picking tea, while Sichuan Opera is famous for how actors change face masks as if by magic. What all these variations share in common is the power to command attention. "This type of theater has music and dance, acting and special effects," Dr. Liu says. "The combination of everything is so striking that people cannot help being pulled into the history and the splendor of the performance."

The costumes are also spectacular. Some opera forms include actors wearing dramatic masks and pantomiming their roles. Others use full-face makeup that transforms an actor into a god or ghost. Specific colors and shapes convey character traits—such as red for loyalty, yellow or blue for fierceness, and heavy white face paint for wickedness.

Peking Opera is the most famous style. It began when several regional troupes came to Beijing in 1790 to perform for the emperor's eightieth birthday. The capital was the perfect environment for theater to flourish. With more than a million residents, the city bustled with urban merchants, civil-service applicants, and others who could frequent the teahouses where troupes performed. The capital also had

Top: This actor portrays the heavenly worm, one of twenty-eight animal constellations in the night sky. *Bottom:* Notes on the guide indicate that this actor would cover his bare chin with a long beard.

plenty of poor young men who considered a career on the stage to be a step up in social status.

In those days, only men could perform onstage or watch in the audience. The plays offered stories of romance, adventure, humor, intrigue, and battle. Story lines also questioned power and broke taboos. Playhouses became important places to exchange gossip and ideas, but the Qing court worried about such hotbeds for trouble in its capital city. It tried to exercise control by sponsoring court operas, banning specific performers and operatic styles, and forbidding officials of certain ranks to attend commercial playhouses. Mostly these edicts were ignored. Beginning in the 1850s, however, the chaos of current events distracted actors, audiences, and rulers alike from the glittering stage lights.

The golden age of opera in Beijing ended by 1900, but the art form is still considered a national treasure. "The opera has survived many political changes," Dr. Liu explains, "It is firmly in the fabric of Chinese culture."

For hundreds of thousands of years, Paleolithic nomads barely changed China's landscape. About ten thousand years ago, people living in more permanent settlements began a dramatic transformation.

第一章

CHAPTER ONE

Yet there is no one single China. This nation encompasses vast deserts, rugged mountains, fertile plains, coastal lowlands, and tropical rain forests. Its people include fifty-six recognized minority groups with unique stories and customs. China's peoples have repeatedly stitched together this patchwork of landscapes and cultural traditions—and for centuries, the empire was more organized and powerful than Western societies.

The results were not always seamless. As everywhere else, the peoples of China have confronted weak government, warlords, famine, and foreign invasion. They also have navigated trade routes, changing technologies, new ideas about how society should work, and massive shifts in political power. Nothing about China's history was predestined. Rather, it is the result of people responding to life's opportunities and challenges, striving to balance tradition and change.

People are perhaps most familiar with China's history of the last century. This book focuses on the seven thousand years that came before. Taking a longer view highlights how modern lives compare to those of past peoples—and reveals how intertwined China's history is with the rest of the world.

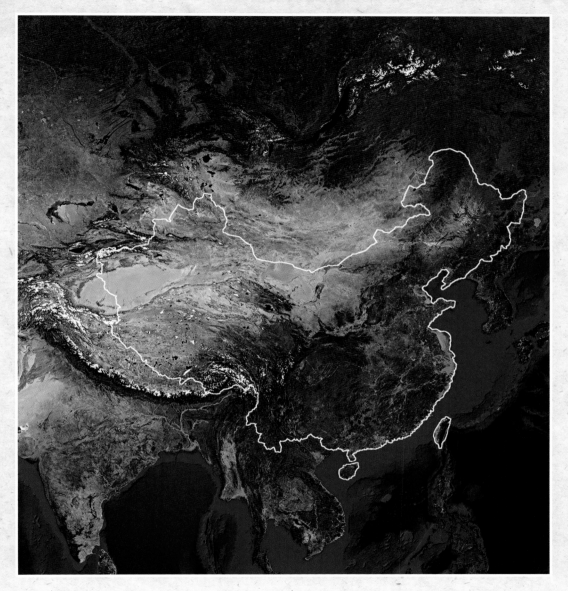

As the world's fourth-largest country by area, China (outlined in white above) is a collage of diverse landscapes and peoples.

并不单一的中国

THERE IS NO SINGLE CHINA

China is the world's fourth-largest country and home to one-fifth of its population. It also has the world's oldest, ongoing tradition of urban civilization.

Starting around 1600 BC, the Shang Dynasty in China ruled over a territory that rivaled what was ruled by Egyptian pharaohs of the time. Since then the pharaohs have fallen, Greek and Roman empires have come and gone, and other ancient cultures have been fundamentally changed by political, religious, and social upheavals. Meanwhile, China's rulers created an empire that persevered until the twentieth century. Then, even after the last emperor was overthrown, China's borders remained mostly unchanged and many Chinese cultural traditions have been largely maintained.

China's history is the story of people responding to opportunities and challenges, striving to balance tradition and change.

绪
论

INTRODUCTION

事
件
表

TIME LINE

Events pertaining to China are in **bold**.

18,000 BC	**Oldest known pottery created in China**
11,000 BC	Clovis people make distinctive spearheads in North America
8500 BC	Sheep first domesticated in Southwest Asia
8000 BC	Oldest evidence of cooking with pottery in Middle East
7000 BC	**Pigs first domesticated in East Asia**
5500 BC	Llamas and alpacas domesticated in South America
3500 BC	Sumerians inscribe cuneiform, the earliest known form of writing, onto clay tablets

3200 BC	Egyptians begin writing with hieroglyphs
3100 BC	Stonehenge built in England
2750 BC	Oldest-known silk fragments created in China
2500 BC	Great Sphinx built in Egypt
2000 BC	Oldest-known noodles created in China
1750 BC	Bullring sports give rise to ancient Greek Minotaur myth
1200 BC	Shang Dynasty writing on oracle bones in China
1046 BC	Zhou rulers introduce first metal coins
776 BC	First Olympics in ancient Greece
700 BC	By now, ancient Greek Homer has written the *Odyssey*
623 BC	Buddha born in Nepal
604 BC	Lao-tzu born in China
551 BC	Confucius born in China
550 BC	First Persian Empire begins
500 BC	By now, blast furnaces invented in China, making cast iron possible
447 BC	Parthenon built in Athens, Greece
221 BC	Qin Shi Huangdi becomes first emperor of China
206 BC	Liu Bang founds Han Dynasty, China's longest imperial dynasty

44 BC	Julius Caesar's death; rise of the Roman Empire
30 AD	Jesus of Nazareth crucified on the cross
105 AD	By now, paper invented in China
200 AD	Overland Silk Road trade routes gaining importance
250 AD	Mayans build pyramids in Central America
476 AD	Roman Empire crumbles
571 AD	Mohammed, founder of Islam, born in Mecca
600 AD	Numerals used today developed in India
618 AD	Tang Dynasty begins
850 AD	By now, gunpowder invented in China
960 AD	Song Dynasty begins
1000 AD	Overland Silk Road trade routes begin to decline
1000 AD	Viking Leif Erikson reaches North America
1050 AD	Printing from moveable type has been invented in China
1066 AD	After Battle of Hastings, William the Conqueror founds line of English royalty
1140 AD	Hindu temple Angkor Wat built in Cambodia
1206 AD	Genghis Khan founds Mongolian Empire
1279 AD	Mongols found the Yuan Dynasty; China becomes part of world's largest empire ever
1299 AD	Ottoman Empire begins in the Middle East

1325 AD	Emperor Mansa Musa I of Mali controls gold mines of tremendous wealth
1368 AD	**Beginning of Ming Dynasty, famous for renovating Forbidden City imperial complex and for maritime sea expeditions**
1441 AD	African slaves begin being transported across Atlantic
1450 AD	Incan Empire builds Machu Picchu
1455 AD	Gutenberg introduces printing press in Europe
1492 AD	Christopher Columbus sails to Americas
1503 AD	Leonardo da Vinci paints the *Mona Lisa*
1513 AD	**Portuguese land in China, eventually negotiate limited trade rights**
1514 AD	Copernicus proposes that Earth revolves around the sun
1519 AD	Spanish defeat Aztec Empire
1620 AD	The *Mayflower* lands at Plymouth Rock in Massachusetts
1644 AD	**Manchu found the Qing Dynasty, China's last imperial dynasty**
1769 AD	James Cook maps the coastline of New Zealand
1771 AD	First water-powered cotton mill opens in Britain
1776 AD	United States declares independence from Britain

1793 AD	Emperor Qianlong complains to King George III about British selling opium in China
1804 AD	Napoleon Bonaparte becomes emperor of France
1839 AD	Lin Zexu destroys opium smuggled into a Chinese port; Opium Wars begin
1850 AD	Taiping Rebellion overthrows Manchu rulers in China
1865 AD	Civil War ends in United States
1869 AD	Transcontinental railroad crosses United States
1898 AD	Marie Curie discovers radioactivity
1899 AD	Boxer Rebellion in China
1912 AD	China's last emperor removed from the throne
1914 AD	Panama Canal built
1914 AD	World War I begins
1939 AD	World War II begins
1949 AD	The Communist Party, led by Mao Zedong, creates the People's Republic of China
1972 AD	President Richard Nixon visits China
2008 AD	Beijing hosts the Olympics

注释

NOTES

5   "Somewhat dejected," he later wrote: Johan Gunnar Andersson, *Children of the Yellow Earth: Studies in Prehistoric China* (Cambridge, MA: MIT Press, 1973), 165.

10   "Having a vessel to carry things": All Deborah Bekken quotes from January 2016 telephone interviews with author.

19   "I've seen people ride by on bikes": All Gary Feinman quotes from January 2016 telephone interviews with author.

36   "Bronze production during this era": Lisa C. Niziolek, Deborah A. Bekken, and Gary M. Feinman, eds., *China: Visions Through the Ages* (Chicago: University of

Chicago Press, 2017), chapter 4, "The Bronze Age in China: What and When." Also email correspondence between the author and Dr. Yung-ti Li, March 2016 to June 2017.

45 "Now today the Emperor has unified": Martin Kern and Ch'in Shih-Huang, *The Stele Inscriptions of Ch'in Shih-Huang: Text and Ritual in Early Chinese Imperial Representation* (New Haven, CT: American Oriental Society, 2000).

50 "You have long suffered": Ssu-ma Ch'ien and William H. Nienhauser Jr., *The Grand Scribe's Records* (Bloomington: Indiana University Press, 2006).

52 "Exceptional work demands exceptional men": John Minford and Joseph S. M. Lau, eds., *Classical Chinese Literature* (New York: Columbia University Press, 2000), 574.

53 "A piece of Chinese plain silk": Valerie Hansen, *The Open Empire: A History of China to 1800* (New York: W. W. Norton, 2015), 123.

62 In the days of the First: Ibid., 47.

64 In the far north there are fast horses: Ibid., 87.

67 "Why must I submit thrice to father": Ibid., 147.

73 "Some have heated together the saltpeter": Jack Kelly, *Gunpowder: Alchemy, Bombards, and Pyrotechnics: The History of the Explosive That Changed the World* (New York: Basic Books, 2005), 8.

81 "Never impose on others": Confucius and David

Hinton, *The Analects* (Berkeley: Counterpoint, 2014), XV.24.

81–82   "To put the world in order": Confucius, *The Great Learning*.

84   "At last I may say that I have seen": Chuang Tzu and Burton Watson, *The Complete Works of Chuang Tzu*, (New York: Columbia University Press, 1968), chapter 14.

84   "Perfect activity leaves no track": Holmes. H. Welch Jr., *Taoism: The Parting of the Way* (Boston: Beacon, 2003), chapter 27, 79.

84   "When the world knows beauty as beauty": Lao-tzu, Trans. Derek Lin, *Tao Te Ching*, chapter 2, www.Taoism.net, accessed on June 20, 2017.

87   "So long as I act only by inactivity": Lao-tzu, Trans. Arthur Waley, *Tao Te ching* (Ware: Wordsworth Editions, 1997), chapter 57, 60.

100   Shadow puppetry was a perfect fit: All Mia Liu quotes from February 2016 telephone interviews.

112–113   "Shipwrecks are an important source": Lisa Niziolek, telephone interview with author, January 16, 2017.

120   "dark, dangerous, and inscrutable": Herbert Allen Giles, *Gems of Chinese Literature* (London: B. Quariteh, 1923).

120   "the tea, silk, and porcelain": *Internet History Sourcebooks*, Fordham University, "Qian Long: Letter to George III, 1793", sourcebooks.fordham.edu accessed on June 20, 2017).

123–124   "are so obsessed with material gain": *Internet History Sourcebooks*, Fordham University, "Commissioner Lin: Letter to Queen Victoria, 1839," sourcebooks.fordham.edu accessed on June 20, 2017).

129   **"People gravitated to theater"**: All Mia Liu quotes from February 2016 telephone interviews with author.

131   **"the true index of the degree"**: Bennet Bronson, "Bertholdt Laufer" in "Curators, Collections, and Contexts: Anthropology at The Field Museum, 1893–2002," Fieldiana Anthropology Publication N. S. 36 (2003): 117–26.

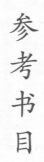

SELECTED BIBLIOGRAPHY

BOOKS

Bekken, Deborah A., Lisa C. Niziolek, and Gary M. Feinman, eds. *China: Visions Through the Ages*. Chicago: University of Chicago Press, 2017.

Ebrey, Patricia Buckley. *Chinese Civilization: A Sourcebook*. New York: Free Press, 1993.

———. *Women and the Family in Chinese History*. London: Routledge, 2003.

Fiskesjö, Magnus, and Xingcan Chen. *China before China: Johan Gunnar Andersson, Ding Wenjiang, and the Discovery of*

China's Prehistory. Stockholm: Museum of Far Eastern Antiquities, 2004.

Hansen, Valerie. *The Open Empire: A History of China to 1800*. New York: W. W. Norton, 2015.

Haw, Stephen G. *A Traveller's History of China*. New York: Interlink, 2014.

Shelach-Lavi, Gideon. *The Archaeology of Early China: From Prehistory to the Han Dynasty.* New York: Cambridge University Press, 2015.

WEBSITES

Cyrus Tang Hall of China Exhibition Online. Chicago: Field Museum, 2015; www.fieldmuseum.org/discover/on-exhibit /china, www.chinahall.fm.

鸣谢

ACKNOWLEDGMENTS

As a writer, and a person of insatiable curiosity, I always relish an opportunity to understand more about our world. I am deeply grateful to The Field Museum for creating the *Cyrus Tang Hall of China* and other exhibitions to explore the diversity of nature and culture on Earth. For this book, particular thanks go to Field Museum archaeologists and exhibition curators Gary Feinman, Deborah Bekken, and Lisa Niziolek for their time and expertise. Tom Skwerski, in the museum's exhibitions department, played a key organizational role. Thanks are due to Dr. Yung-ti Li, of the University of Chicago, and Mia Yinxing Liu, at Bates College, for sharing insights into specific topics. I also thank editor Howard Reeves and the Abrams team, who care so much about creating beautiful books to inspire insatiable curiosity in the next generation of young readers.

插
图
出
处

IMAGE CREDITS

Bean. **Page 8:** from Kwang-Chih Chang, *The Archaeology of Ancient China.* New Haven, Connecticut: Yale University Press, 1986, p. 118. **Page 9:** from "Early Pottery at 20,000 Years Ago in Xianrendong Cave, China," Xiaohong Wu et al., *Science,* June 29, 2012, vol. 336, pp. 1696–1700. **Page 10:** © The Field Museum, catalog no. 118800, photographer Gedi Jakovickas. **Page 11:** Tomasz Resiak, via Flickr. **Page 12:** (*top left*) © The Field Museum, photo ID no. GN92035_016d, photographer Karen Bean; (*bottom right*) courtesy of Professor Fang Hui and Professor Xuexiang Chen, Shandong University, China. **Pages 13, 27** (*top left*): courtesy The Hemudu Site Museum. **Page 14:** © The Field Museum, uncatalogued, photographer Gedi Jakovickas. **Page 15:** © The Field Museum, catalog nos. 182932, 182915, 182988, 183033, 182940, 183038, photographer Gedi Jakovickas. **Page 16:** (*top left*) © The Field Museum, catalog nos. 116577, 1165778, photographer Gedi Jakovickas; (*bottom left*) © The Field Museum, catalog nos. 182677, 183456, photographer Gedi Jakovickas; (*bottom right*) courtesy Museum of Far Eastern Asian Art in

Stockholm, Sweden. **Page 17:** © The Field Museum, photo ID no. GN92118_058D, photographer Karen Bean. **Pages 18, 19, 20, 50:** Images courtesy of Linda Nicholas. **Pages 22, 23, 26** (*top right*), **39** (*bottom left*), **48:** (*top*), **54:** © The Field Museum, illustrator Sayaka Isowa. **Page 25:** © The Field Museum, photo ID no. GN92128_010D, photographer Karen Bean. **Page 26:** (*top left*) © The Field Museum, catalog no. 235889, photographer Gedi Jakovickas. **Page 27:** (*top right*) courtesy of Chinese Academy of Science. **Page 28:** image © DESIGNBOOM. **Page 32:** © The British Library Board, B20086-05 OR. 11515, F. 11V. **Pages 34, 47** (*bottom left*): The Trustees of the British Museum. **Page 36:** (*left*) © The Field Museum, catalog no. 117377, photographer Gedi Jakovickas; (*right*) © The Field Museum, catalog nos. 181601, 181602, photographer Gedi Jakovickas. **Page 37:** © The Field Museum, illustrator Sayaka Isowa, from *The Great Bronze Age of China,* New York: Alfred A. Knopf, 1980, p. 72. **Page 38:** (*top*) courtesy Feng Zhong, via Flickr; (*bottom*) © The Field Museum, catalog no. 232992, photographer Gedi Jakovickas. **Page 39:** (*top*) © The Field

Museum, catalog nos. 121061, 121062, 121063, photographer Gedi Jakovickas. **Page 40:** © The Field Museum, catalog nos. 124503, 124500, 124504, photographer Gedi Jakovickas. **Page 41:** © The Field Museum, catalog nos. 116743, 116755, photographer Gedi Jakovickas. **Page 42:** © The Field Museum, photo ID no. A3606, catalog no. 121488, photographer Karen Bean. **Page 44:** © The Field Museum, illustrator Erica Rodriguez. **Page 45:** © The Field Museum, illustrator Jeff Busch. **Page 46:** © The Field Museum, catalog no. 341421, photographer Gedi Jakovickas. **Page 47:** (*top*) courtesy of the National Museum of China; (*bottom right*) image in public domain. **Page 48:** (*bottom*) © RMN-Grand Palais/Art Resource, New York. **Page 49:** © 123RF, Chuyu. **Page 51:** Image in public domain, via Wikimedia Commons, by Yan Li-pen. **Page 52:** © The Field Museum, photo ID no. A115104D_004, catalog no. 233471, photographer Karen Bean. **Page 53:** image in public domain, via Wikimedia Commons, Song Yingxing, Tiangong Kaiwu, AD 1637. **Page 55:** (*top, bottom*) Examination Hall, Sidney D. Gamble Photographs, David M. Rubenstein

Rare Book and Manuscript Library, Duke University, Durham, North Cariolina. **Page 56:** © The Field Museum, photo ID no. A115189D_002, catalog no. 217678, photographer Karen Bean. **Page 57:** image in public domain, via Wikimedia Commons. **Pages 58–59:** (*bottom*) image in public domain, via Wikimedia Commons, courtesy Liaoning Provincial Museum, Shenyang. **Page 59:** (*top*) image in public domain, via Wikimedia Commons, courtesy Chris Gyford. **Page 60:** © The Field Museum, photo ID no. A115148D_006, catalog no. 114340, photographer Karen Bean. **Page 62:** © The Field Museum, catalog no. 127037, photographer Gedi Jakovickas. **Pages 63** (*top, bottom*), **64** (*bottom*): Henan Provincial Institute of Cultural Relics and Archaeology, courtesy of Dr. T. R. Kidder, Washington University, St. Louis, Missouri. **Page 65:** courtesy of Joriz De Guzman. **Page 66:** image in public domain. **Page 68:** (*top*) courtesy of Wellcome Library; (*bottom*) courtesy Ralph Repo. **Page 69:** (*top left*) image in public domain, from Ming Chuang-Yuan T'u-K'ao, 1607 edition; (*top right*) © The Field Museum, photo ID no.

GN92102_039D, photographer Karen Bean. **Page 70:** (*top left*) © The Field Museum, catalog no. 118030, photographer Gedi Jakovickas; (*top right*) © The Field Museum, catalog no. 253317, photographer Gedi Jakovickas. **Page 71:** (*top left*) The Field Museum, photo ID no. A115060D_005, catalog no. 127481, photographer Karen Bean; (*top right*) © The Field Museum, A114607_051d, photographer Karen Bean. **Page 72:** (*top left*) courtesy Wang Lu/ Chinastock; (*top right*) © The Field Museum, A115192D_024, catalog no. 119614, photographer Karen Bean; (*bottom right*) © The Field Museum, A115192D_047, catalog no. 119614, photographer Karen Bean. **Page 73:** (*top left*) © The Field Museum, catalog no. 121976, photographer Gedi Jakovickas; (*top right*) © Musee Conde, Chantilly, France/Bridgeman Images. **Page 74:** (*top left*) ©The Field Museum, catalog no. 120985, photographer Gedi Jakovickas; (*top right*) © The Field Museum, catalog nos. 124579, 124639, 124648, 124560, 116945, 124596, 116929, 124507, 124757.2, 124750, photographer Gedi Jakovickas. **Page 78:** © The Field Museum, photo ID no.

A115150d_004A, catalog no. 121224, photographer Karen Bean. **Page 80:** (*top*) © The Field Museum, A115161d_003, catalog no. 244853, photographer Karen Bean; (*bottom*) © The Field Museum, A115099D_004, catalog no. 27465, photographer Karen Bean. **Page 83:** © The Field Museum, A115159D, catalog no. 244344, photographer Karen Bean. **Page 85:** © The Field Museum, catalog nos. 127941, 127942, 127943, 127944, 127937, 127938, 127939, 127940, photographer Gedi Jakovickas. **Pages 86–87:** courtesy Shaanxi Cultural Heritage Promotion Center. **Page 88:** courtesy of Will Clayton, via Flickr. **Page 90:** © HANHANPEGGY, Dreamstime.com, ID 4303180. **Page 91:** © The Field Museum, catalog nos. 121480, 121485, photographer Gedi Jakovickas. **Page 93:** © The Field Museum, photo ID no. A115167d_002, catalog no. 233247, photographer Karen Bean. **Page 95:** (*left*) © The Field Museum, catalog no. 119332, photographer John Weinstein; (*right*) © The Field Museum, catalog no. 120263, photographer Gedi Jakovickas. **Page 96:** courtesy Ana Paula Hirama, via Flickr. **Page 98:** (*top left*) © The Field Museum, catalog no.

244395, photographer Gedi Jakovickas; (*bottom right*) © The Field Museum, catalog no. 358205, photographer Sarah Crawford. **Page 99:** (*top left*) © The Field Museum, catalog no. 120981, photographer Gedi Jakovickas; (*top right*) © The Field Museum, photo ID no. A115105D_007, catalog no. 245063, photographer Karen Bean. **Page 100:** © The Field Museum, catalog no. 120889, photographer Gedi Jakovickas. **Page 101:** (*top*) © The Field Museum, catalog no. 120930, 120931, 120927, 120929, 120932, photographer Gedi Jakovickas; (*bottom*) © The Field Museum, photographer Greg Mercer. **Page 104:** Wolfgang Kaehler. **Page 107:** ©The Field Museum, Illustrator David Quednau. **Page 108:** © The British Library Board. **Page 109:** © The Field Museum, catalog no. 255637, photographer Gedi Jakovickas. **Page 111:** courtesy Bibliothèque Nationale de France. **Page 112:** © Archivo Arqua © Pacific Sea Resources, Inc. **Page 114:** © The Field Museum, photographer Scott Demel. **Page 116:** © The Field Museum, catalog no. 357836, photographer Gedi Jakovickas. **Page 117:** courtesy beibaoke/shutterstock.com. **Page 119:**

© DeAgostini Picture Library/W. Buss/Bridgeman Images. **Page 121:** © The Field Museum, catalog no. 125834, photographer Gedi Jakovickas. **Pages 122–123:** © Brown University Library, Providence, Rhode Island/Bridgeman Images. **Pages 125, 127, 128:** © Pictures from History/ Bridgeman Images. **Page 126:** © Private Collection Archives Charmet/ Bridgeman Images. **Page 129:** © The Field Museum. photo ID no. A115012d, catalog no. 121900, photographer John Weinstein. **Page 130:** (*top*) © The Field Museum. photo ID no. A115013d, catalog no. 121901, photographer John Weinstein; (*bottom*) © The Field Museum. photo ID no. A115014d, catalog no. 121905, photographer John Weinstein. **Page 131:** (*top*) © The Field Museum, photo ID no. CSA49114; (*bottom*) © The Field Museum, photo ID no. A98299. **Page 134:** © The Field Museum, photo ID no. A114786d_004, catalog no. 244810, photographer John Weinstein. **Page 136:** courtesy of wuqiang_beijing, via Wikimedia Commons. **Page 137:** © Omniphoto/ UIG/Bridgeman Images. **Page 138:** © The Field Museum, photo ID no. GN92138_017d, photographer Karen Bean.

INDEX

Page numbers in *italics* refer to illustrations.

INDEX